English Urdu
Word to Word Dictionary

لـ غت

Wasim Salaamat
and
Nazia Rizvi

Title: English Urdu Word to Word Dictionary
Author: Wasim Salaamat and Nazia Rizvi
Layout: Peterson Joseph

For more information, please contact:

Educa Vision Inc.
2725 NW 19th Street,
Pompano Beach, FL 33069
Telephone: (954) 968-7433
E-mail: educa@aol.com
Web: www.educavision.com

Introduction

Standard Urdu, is a South Asian language. It is the national language of Pakistan. It is also an official language of five Indian states and one of the 22 languages in the Constitution of India. Urdu is mutually intelligible with Standard Hindi spoken in India. Both languages share the same base, and are similar in basic structure, grammar and to a large extent vocabulary and phonology. The combined population of Urdu and Standard Hindi speakers is the fourth largest in the world.

This bilingual version of the English-Urdu Word to Word Dictionary focuses on words, that are relevant for students taking school exams. The entries are in English and their equivalents are presented in both Urdu scripts and in Roman Urdu. This tool is a pragmatic help for ELL students to take exams and it also facilitate communication between Urdu and English speakers. It contains more than 19,000 entries.

A

Abandoned Adjective`	چھوڑی ہوئی	chhori hui
Abandonment noun	ترک	tark
Abandonment noun	دست برداری	dastbardaari
Abase verb	ذلیل کرنا	zaleel karna
Abasement noun	ذلت	zillat
Abash verb; to abash	شرمندہ کرنا	sharminda karna
Abash verb; to be abashed	شرمانا	sharmaana
Abashment noun	شرمندگی	sharmindagi
Abate verb	کم کرنا	kam karna
Abatement noun	کمی	kami
Abbess	پادرن	paadran
Abbey noun	خانقاہ	khaan-kaah
Abbot	پادری	padri
Abbreviate verb	مخفف	Mukhafaf
Abbreviation noun	خلاصہ	khulaasa

Abbreviation noun	مختصر	mukhtasar
Abdicate verb	تخت چھوڑنا	takht chhorna
Abdication noun	تخت سے علیحدگی	takht say alehdagi
Abdomen noun	پیٹ	pait
Abdominal noun	پیٹ کا	pait ka
Abduct verb	اغوا کرنا	aghwa karna
Abduction noun	اغوا	aghwa
Abductor noun	اغوا کرنے والا	aghwa karnay wala
Abdullah noun; male name	عبداللھ	abdullah
Abed	بستر میں	bister mein
Aberrance	گمراہی	gumraahi
Aberrancy	گمراہی	gumraahi
Aberrant	گمراہ	gumraah
Aberration	گمراہی	gumraahi
Abet verb	مجرم کی مدد کرنا	mujrim ki madad karna
Abetment noun	اعانت	aiyanat

Abettor noun	مددگار جرم	madadgaar-e-jurm
Abeyance noun	عارضی التوا	aarzi iltewa
Abhor verb	نفرت کرنا	nafrat karna
Abhorrence noun	نفرت	nafrat
Abhorrent adjective	مکروہ	makruh
Abhorrer adjective	نفرت کرنے والا	nafrat karnay wala
abid noun; name	عابد	abid
Abide verb	تسلیم کرنا	tasleem karna
Abiding adjective	پائیدار	paidaar
Ability noun	قابلیت	qaabliyat
Ability noun	صلاحیت	salaahiyat
Abject adjective	کم تر	kam tar
Abjection noun	کم تری	kamtari
Abjuration noun	حلف دست برداری	halaf-e-dastbardaari
Abjure verb	انکاری قسم کھانا	inkaari qasam khaana
Ablaze adjective	دہکتا	dehekta

Able adjective	قابل	qaabil
Able adjective	لائق	laik
Ablebodied adjective	عام جسمانی صلاحیت	aam jismani slahiyat
Abloom adjective	شگفتہ	shagufta
Ablution noun	غسل	ghusal
Abnegate verb	پرہیز کرنا	parhayz karnaa
Abnegation	پرہیز	parhez
Abnormal	خلاف معمول	khilaaf-e-mamool
Abnormity	بے اعتدالی	bay-ay'tedaali
Aboard	جہاز پر	jahaaz par
Abode	گھر	ghar
Abolish	منسوخ کرنا	mansookh karnaa
abominable adjective	نفرت انگیز	nafrat angez
Abortion	اسقاط حمل	asqaat-e-hamal
Abortive	ناقص	naa-qis
Abound intr. verb; to be plentiful	بکثرت ہونا	ba-kasrat honaa
About preposition; around	گرد	gird

About preposition; nearby	آس پاس	aas paas
About adverb	تقریباً	taqreeban
About preposition; concerning	بارے میں	baaray mein
Above	اوپر	oopar
Abreast adverb	ساتھ ساتھ	saat saat
Abridge	مختصر کرنا	mukhtasir karnaa
Abridgement	اختصار	ikhtesaar
Abroad	باہر	baahir
Abrupt	اچانک	achaanak
Abruptly	ایک دم سے	aik dum say
Absence	غیرحاضری	ghair haazari
Absent	غایب	ghaaib
Absolute	قطعی	qatai
Absorb	جزب کرنا	jazb karnaa
Abstain verb; keep oneself away	باز رہنا	baaz rehna
Abstract	خلاصہ	khulaasa

Abstruse	مشکل	mushkil
Absurd	بے معنی	bay-maa'ni
Abundance	کثرت	kasrat
Abundant	بکثرت	bakasrat
Abuse verb; wrong use	غلط استعمال	ghalat istaymaal
Abuse verb; maltreatment	برا برتاؤ	buraa bartaao
Abyss	پاتال	paa-taal
Acacia	کیکر	keekar
Academy	مدرسہ	madarasa
Accelerate	تیز کرنا	tez karnaa
Acceleration	تیز رفتاری	tayz raftaari
Accelerator noun	پائدان زود رفتار	Paeedaan-e-zood-e-raftar
Accent	لہجہ	lehjaa
Accentuate	واضح کرنا	waazeh karnaa
Accept verb	منظور کرنا	manzoor karna
Acceptable adjective	قابل قبول	qaabil-e-qabool
Acceptance noun	منظوری	manzoori

Acceptation	مقبولیت	maqbooliyat
Accepted adjective	تسلیم شدہ	tasleem shudaa
Access noun	پہنچ	pohanch
Accessary noun	مدد گار جرم	madadgaar e jurm
Accessible	قابل پہنچ	qabil-e-pohanch
Accession noun	تخت نشینی	takht nasheeni
Accessory noun	مدد گار جرم	madadgaar e jurm
Accessory noun	پرزے	purzay
Accident	حادثہ	haadsa
Acclaim	تسلیم کرنا	tasleem karnaa
Acclivity	بلندی	bulandi
Accolade	شاباش	shaabaash
Accolade	واہ واہ	waah-waah
Accolades	شاباش	shaabaash
Accommodate	جگہ بنانا	jagaah banaana
Accommodation	قیام گاہ	qayyaam gaah
Accompany	ہمراہ ہونا	hamraah honaa
Accomplice	شریک	shareek

Accomplish verb	پورا کرنا	pooraa karnaa
Accomplishment noun	کامیابی	kaamyaabi
Accord	سات دینا	saath dena
Accordance	منتفق	muntafiq
According	مطابق	mutaabik
Accordingly	اس واسطے	is waastay
Accost	مخاطب کرنا	mukhaatib karnaa
Account	حساب کتاب	hisaab kitaab
Accountable	ذمہ دار	zimadaar
Accountant	محاسب	muhaasib
Accounting noun	حساب کاری	hesab kari
Accoutrement	سازوسامان	saz-o-saamaan
Accoutrements	سازوسامان	saz-o-samaan
Accredit verb	منظور کرنا	manzoor karnaa
Accreditation	اجازتنامہ	ijaazat naama
Accrue	پیدا کرنا	peda karnaa
Accumulate verb	جمع کرنا	jamaa karnaa

Accumulation noun	ڈھیر	dhayr
Accuracy	درستگی	durust'gi
Accurate adjective	صحیح	sahih
Accurately	درستگی سے	durust'gi say
Accursed	مردود	mardood
Accusation	الزام	ilzaam
Accuse	الزام لگانا	ilzaam lagaana
Accused	ملزم	mulzim
Accustom	عادی	aadi
Ache	درد	dard
Achieve verb	انجام دینا	anjaam dayna
Achievement noun	کامیابی	kaamyaabi
Aching	درد کرنا	dard karnaa
Acid	تیزاب	tezaab
Acidity	تیزابیت	tezaabiyat
Acknowledge	تسلیم کرنا	tasleem karnaa
Acknowledgement	منظوری	manzoori

Acme	بہترین	behtareen
Acorn	بلوط	baloot
Acquaint	آگاہ ہونا	aagaah hona
Acquaintance	جان پہچان	jaan-pehchaan
Acquainted	واقف	waaqif
Acquire	حاصل کرنا	haasil karnaa
Acquisition	حصول	hasool
Acquit	رہا کرنا	rihaa karnaa
Across	پار	paar
Act	عمل کرنا	amal karnaa
Acting	اداکاری کرنا	adakaari karnaa
Action noun; process	کاروائی	kaarwai
Action noun; work	فعل	fayl
Action noun; influence	اثر	asar
Activate verb; to activate	چلانا	chalaanaa
Activate verb; to be activated	چلنا	chalnaa
Active adjective; energetic	پھرتیلا	phurteela

Active adjective; turned on	چلتا	chaltaa
activity noun	مشق	Mashq
Actor	اداکار	adaakaar
Actress	اداکارہ	adaakaara
Actual adjective; real	اصلی	aslee
Actuality noun	اصلیت	asleeyat
Actually adverb	حقیقتاً	haqeeqatan
Actuate	تحریک کرنا	tehreek karnaa
Acute	شدت	shiddat
Adage	کہاوت	kahawat
Adapt	اپنانا	apnaana
Adaptation	اپنانا	ap'naana
Add verb; unite	جوڑنا	jorhna
Add verb; introduce	شامل کرنا	shaamil karna
Addendum	اضافہ	izaafaa
Addict noun	عادی	aadi
Addicted adjective	عادی	aadi

Addiction noun	عادت	aadat
Addition noun	اضافہ	izaafaa
Additional adjective	اضافی	izaafi
Address verb	خطاب کرنا	khitaab karna
Address noun; formal talk	خطبہ	khutbaa
Address noun; location	پتا	pataa
Addressee noun	مکتوب الیہ	maktoob ilayh
Adduce	ثبوت دینا	sabooth denaa
Adept	ماہر	maahir
Adequate	مناسب	munaasib
Adequately	پورے طور پر	pooray taur par
Adhere	ثابت قدم رہنا	sabit qadam rehnaa
Adherent	چسپاں	chaspaan
Adhesive	چپکنےوالا	chipaknay wala
Adjacent	متصل	muttasil
Adjective	صفت	sift
Adjoin	متصل	mutassil

Adjoining	جڑا ہوا	jura huwa
Adjourn	ملتوی کرنا	multawi karnaa
Adjudge	فیصلہ کرنا	faysala karnaa
Adjust	ٹھیک کرنا	thheek karnaa
Adjustment	ترتیب	tarteeb
Administer	انتظام کرنا	intezaam karnaa
Administration	انتظام	intezaam
Administration	انتظامیہ	intezaamia
Administrator	منتظم	muntazim
Admirable	قابل تعریف	qabil-e-taa'reef
Admiral	امیر البحر	ameer-ul-beher
Admiration	تعریف	taareef
Admire	تعریف کرنا	ta'reef karnaa
Admission	داخلہ	daakhlaa
Admit	داخل کرنا	daakhil karnaa
Admonish	تاکید کرنا	taakeed karnaa
Admonition	تاکید	taakeed

Adnan noun; name	عدنان	Adnan
Adolescence	جوانی	jawaani
Adopt	اختیار کرنا	ikhteyaar karnaa
Adoption	اپنانا	apnaana
Adorable	پیارا	piraara
Adoration	محبت	muhabbat
Adore	پسند کرنا	pasand karnaa
Adorn	آراستہ کرنا	araasta karnaa
Adrift	بہتا ہوا	behtaa huwaa
Adulation	خوشامد کرنا	khushaamad karnaa
Adult	بالغ	baligh
Advance	آگے بڑھنا	aagay barna
Advancement	ترقی	taraqqi
Advantage	فائدہ	faidaa
Advantageous	مفید	mufeed
Advent	آمد	aamad
Adventure	پرہمت مہم	pur-himmat muhim

Adventurous	جانباز	jaanbaaz
Adverb	متعلق فعل	mutallak fayl
Adversary	مخالف	mukhaalif
Adverse	خلاف	khilaaf
Advert	حوالہ دینا	hawaala dena
Advertise	اشتہار دینا	ishtehaar dena
Advertisement noun	اشتہار	ishtayhaar
Advice	نصیحت	naseehat
Advise	نصیحت کرنا	naseehat karnaa
Advisory	مشاورتی	mashaawarti
Advocacy	وکالت	wakaalat
Advocate	وکیل	wakeel
Aerial	ہوائی	hawaai
Aeronaut	ہوا باز	hawaa-baaz
aeroplane transport	ہوائی جہاز	hwai jahaz
Affair	ماجرہ	majaarah
Affect	اثر کرنا	asar karnaa

Affection	محبت	muhabbat
Affectionate	شفیق	shafeeq
Affective	موئثر	mo'assar
Affidavit	اظہار	iz-haar
Affiliate	ساتھی	saathi
Affiliation	تعلق	taa'luq
Affinity	قرابت	qaraabat
Affirm	تاکید کرنا	taakeed karnaa
Affirmation	اقرار	iqraar
Affix	لگانا	lagaana
Afflict verb	تکلیف میں ڈالنا	takleef mein daalnaa
Affliction noun	تکلیف	takleef
Afford	گنجائش	gunjaish
affordable adjective	قابل برداشت	qabil e berdaasht
Afloat	تیرتا ہوا	tayrtaa huwaa
Afraid adjective	خوف زدہ	khofzadaa
Africa	افریقہ	africa

After preposition; later	بعد	baad
After preposition; behind	پیچھے	peechhay
Aftermath	انجام	an'jaam
Afternoon	سہ پہر	sa-peher
Afterwards	اس کے بعد	is kay baad
Again adverb	دوبارہ	dobaaraa
Against preposition	خلاف	khilaaf
Age	عمر	umer
Age	زمانہ	zamana
Aged	ضعیف	za'eef
Agency	وسیلہ	waseela
Agent	گماشتہ	gamaashtaa
Aggregate	جمع کرنا	ja'maa karnaa
Aggregation	اجتماع	ij'tamaa
Aggression	چڑھائی	charhaai
Aggressive	جنگجو	jang ju
Aggressor	جنگ آور	jang aawaar

Aggrieve	دکھ دینا	dukh dena
Aghast	خوفزدا	khof zadaa
Agile	پھرتیلا	phurteela
Agility	پھرتی	phurti
Agitate	حرکت کرنا	harkat karnaa
Agitation	احتجاج	aihtijaaj
Agnostic	ملحد	mulhid
Agnosticism	الحاد	ilhaad
Ago	گذشتہ	guzishta
Agonize	سخت تکلیف دینا	sakht takleef dena
Agony	سخت تکلیف	sakht takleef
Agree	متفق ہونا	muttafiq hona
Agreement	معاہدہ	mu'aahida
Agriculture	زراعت	zaraa'at
Aground	زمین پر	zameen par
Ague	سردی کا بخار	sardi ka bukhaar
Ahead	آگے	aagay

ahmed noun; name	احمد	ahmed
Aid	مدد	madad
Ail	بیمار ہونا	bimaar hona
Ailment	تکلیف	takleef
Aim	نشانہ	nishaana
Air	ہوا	hawa
Airplane	ہوائی جہاز	hawaai jahaz
Airport	ہوائی اڈہ	hawaai adda
Airy	ہوا دار	hawaa daar
Ajar	کھلا ہوا	khulaa huwa
Akin	رشتہ دار	rishtedaar
Alarm	انتباہ	intebaah
Alarming	خوف ناک	khofnaak
Alas	افسوس	afsos
Album	البم	album
Alcohol	شراب	sharaab
Alert	ہوشیار	hoshyaar

Ali noun	علی	ali
Alias noun	لقب	laqab
Alien	اجنبی	ajnabi
Alienate	الگ کرنا	alag karna
Alight	روشن	roshan
Alike	یکساں	yaksaan
Aliment	خوراک	khoraak
Alive	زندہ	zindaa
Alkali	القلی	al-qali
All adjective	تمام	tamaam
Allah	اللہ	allah
allegation noun	الزام	ilzam
Allege	الزام دینا	ilzaam dena
Alleged	منسوب کردہ	mansoob karda
Allegiance	تابعداری	taabedari
Alleviate	کم کرنا	kam karna
Alleviation	تخفیف	tekh-feef

Alley	گلی	gali
Alliance	معاہدہ	muaahida
Alligator	مگرمچ	magar mach
Allocate	مقرر کرنا	muqarrar karna
Allocation	مقررہ	muqarara
Allot	دینا	dena
Allotment	حصہ	hissa
Allow	اجازت دینا	ijazat dena
Allow	اجازت دینا	ijazat dena (new)
Allowance	تنخواہ	tankhoa
Alloy	مرکب دھات	murakab-e-dhat
Allude	اشارہ کہنا	ishaaraa kehna
Allure	ورغلانا	warghalaana
Allurement	دھوکہ	dhoka
Allusion	بھید	bhed
Alluvial	ذرخیز	zarkhez
Alluvium	سیلابی مٹی	selaabi mitti
Ally	اتحادی	itehaadi

Almanac	تقویم	taqveem
Almighty	قادر	qaadir
Almighty	مطلق	mutliq
Almond	بادام	baadaam
Almost	تقریباً	taqreeban
Alms	خیرات	khairaat
Aloft	بلند	buland
Alone adverb	اکیلے	akaylay
Alone adjective; unique	اکیلا	akaylaa
Alone adjective; without company	تنہا	tanhaa
Along	ساتھ ساتھ	saath saath
Along preposition	بمعہ	Bama
Aloof	علیحدہ	alehda
alot noun	بہت	bohot
Aloud	بلند آواز سے	buland awaaz say
Alphabet	حروف تہجی	haruf-e-tahaji
Alphabetical	با حرف	baa harf

Already adverb	پہلے سے	pehlay say
Alright adverb	ٹھیک	theek
Also	بھی	bhi
Altar	قربان گاہ	qurban gaah
Alter verb	تبدیل کرنا	tabdeel karnaa
Alteration	تبدیلی	tabdeeli
Altercation	بحث	behes
Alternate verb	باری باری	baari baari
Alternative	دوسرا راستہ	dusra raasta
Although	اگرچہ	agar-chay
Altitude	اونچائی	unchaai
Altogether	تمام تر	tamaam-tar
Always adverb	ہمیشہ	hamayshaa
Am	ہوں	hun
Amass	جمع کرنا	jamaa karna
Amateur	شوقین	shoqeen
Amaze	حیران ہونا	hayraan hona

Amazement	حیرانی	hayraani
Amazing	حیران کن	hayraan-kun
Ambassador	سفیر	safeer
Ambiguity	شک	shak
Ambiguous	مشکوک	mashkook
Ambition noun	امنگ	umang
Ambitious	خواہش مند	khuwahish mand
Ambulance	امبولنس	ambulance
Ambush	گھات	ghat
Ameliorate	بہتر کرنا	behtar karna
Amen interjection	آمین	ameen
Amend	دِرست کرنا	durust karna
Amendment	اصلاح	islaah
America noun	امریکا	america
Amiable	خوش مزاج	khush mazaaj
Amid	درمیان	darmiyaan
amir name	امیر	amir

Amiss	غلطی سے	ghalti say
Amity	دوستی	dosti
Ammunition	سامان جنگ	samaan-e-jang
Amnesty noun	عام معافی	aam muafi
Among	درمیان	darmian
Amount	شمار	shumaar
Ample	بہت	bohot
Amply	بھرپور	bharpoor
Amulet	تعویز	taa'veez
Amuse	خوش ہونا	khush hona
Amusement	خوشی	khushi
Amusing	دلچسپ	dilchasp
An	ایک	ek
Analogous	یکساں	yaksaan
Analogy	مشابہت	mushaabihaat
Analysis	تشریح	tashreeh
Ancestor	آبا ؤ اجداد	aabaa-o-ajdaad
Ancestral	آبائی	aabaai

Ancient noun	قدیم	qadeem
And conjunction	اور	aor
Anecdote	واقعہ	waqia
aneesa noun; name	انیسہ	aneesa
Anew	نیا	nia
Angel noun	فرشتہ	farishtaa
Anger noun	غصہ	gussaa
Anger verb	غصہ دلانا	gussaa dilaanaa
Angle	کونا	konaa
Angry adjective	غصے میں	ghussay mein
Anguish	انتہائی تکلیف	intehaai takleef
Animal	جانور	janwar
Animate verb	جان ڈالنا	jaan daalnaa
Animation verb; liveliness	جوش	josh
Animosity	دشمنی	dushmani
Ankle	ٹخنہ	takhna
Annals	تواریخ	tawareekh

Annex	ملانا	milaana
Annexation	جوڑ	jorh
Annihilate	مٹا دینا	mitaa dena
Annihilation	بربادی	barbaadi
Anniversary	سالگرہ	saalgiraah
Annotate	تفسیر کرنا	tafseer karna
Annotation	تفسیر	tafseer
Announce	اعلان کرنا	ilaan karna
Announcement	اعلان	ilaan
Annoy	ستانا	sataana
Annoyance	ناراضگی	naaraaz'gi
annoying adjective	تکلیف دہ	takleef deh
Annual	سالانہ	saalaana
Annuity	سالانہ وظیفہ	salaana wazeefa
Annul	رد کرنا	rad karna
Anoint	مخصوص کرنا	makhsus karna
Anonymous	بےنام	benaam
Another	دوسرا	doosra

Answer	جواب	jawab
Answer	جواب دینا	jawaab dena
Ant	چیونٹی	chuntee
Anthem	ترانہ	taraana
Anthology	بیاض	biaz
Anti	مخالف	mukhalif
Antic noun; clown	مسخرہ	maskhara
Antic noun; pranks	کرتب	kartab
Anticipate	پیشقدمی کرنا	pesh-qadmi karna
Anticipation	پیشقدمی	pesh-qadmi
Antics noun; pranks	کرتب	kartab
Antidote	زہرمار	zeher-maar
Antique	قدیم	qadeem
Antiquity	پرانا زمانہ	puraana zamaana
Antiquity	قدیم	qadeem shay
anxiety noun	بیچینی	be cheni
Anxious adjective; nervous	پریشان	parayshaan

Anxious adjective; eager	بے چین	baychayn
Anxiously	فکرمندی سے	fikarmandi say
Any adjective	کوئی	koi
Anyhow	بہرحال	bahar-haal
Anything pronoun	کچھ بھی	kuch bhi
Anyway adverb	بہر حال	beher haal
Anywhere	کہیں بھی	kahin bhi
Apace	فوراً	foren
Apart	الگ	alag
Apartment	کوٹھی	kothi
Ape	بیدم بندر	bedum bandar
Aperture	سوراخ	suraakh
Apex	بلند ترین مقام	buland tareen maqaam
Apiece	ایک ایک	aik aik
Apocalypse	آخری دن	aakhri din
Apologize verb	معذرت چاہنا	maazarat chaahna
Apology noun	معافی	maafi

Appal	ڈرانا	daraana
Apparatus	آلات	aalaat
Apparel	کپڑے	kaparay
Apparent	ظاہر	zaahir
Apparently	ظاہری طور پر	zaahiri taur par
Apparition	صورت	soorat
Appeal	درخواست	darkhaast
Appear	ظاہر ہونا	zahir hona
Appear	شایع ہونا	shaayaa hona
Appearance	صورت	soorat
Appease	اطمینان دلانا	itmenaan dilaana
Appellant	مرافعہ کرنے والا	murafay karnay waala
Appellation	خطاب	khitaab
Append	جوڑنا	jorhna
Appendix	ضمیمہ	zameema
Appertain	تعلق رکھنا	taa'luq rakhna
Appetite	بھوک	bhook

Applaud	واہ واہ	wah wah
Applause	آفرین	aafreen
Apple noun	سیب	sayb
Appliance	اوزار	ozaar
Applicable adjective	موزوں	mozoon
Applicant	سائل	saa'il
Application noun; request	درخواست	darkhuaast
Application noun; implementation	وسائل کو کام میں لانا	wasail ko kaam mein laanaa
Application noun; spreading liquid	لگانا	lagaana
Apply	درخواست کرنا	darkhaast karna
Appoint	مقرر کرنا	muqarrar karna
Appointment	عہدہ	uhda
Apportion	بانٹنا	baantna
Appraise	اندازہ لگانا	andaaza lagaana
Appreciate	قدر کرنا	qadr karna
Appreciation	قدردانی	qadrdaani

Apprehend	گرفتار کرنا	giriftaar karna
Apprehension	سمجھ	samajh
Apprentice	شاگرد	shagird
Apprise	آگاہ کرنا	agaah karna
Approach	قریب جانا	qareeb jaana
Approbation	تسلیم	tasleem
Appropriate	مناسب	munaasib
Approval noun; good opinion	پسندیدگی	pasandeedgi
Approval noun; acceptance	منظوری	manzoori
Approve verb; liking	پسند کرنا	pasand karnaa
Approve verb; acceptance	تصدیق کرنا	tasdeek karnaa
Approximate	تقریبا	taqreeban
Approximately adjective	تقریباً	taqreeban
Apricot	خبانی	khubaani
April	اپریل	april
Apron	ایپرن	apron
Apt	درست	durust

Aptitude	قابلیت	qaabliat
Aptly	ٹھیک	theek
Aqua	آب	aab
Aquarium	مچھلی گھر	machhli ghar
Aquatic	آبی	aabi
Aqueduct	نالی	naali
Arabic	عربی	arabic
Arable	قابلزراعت	qabil-e-zaraa'at
Arbitrary adjective	خود مختار	khudmukhtaar
Arc	قوس	qos
Archaeology noun	علم آثار قدیمہ	ilm-e-aasaar-e- qadeemaa
Architect	معمار	ma'maar
Architecture	علم تعمیر	ilm-e-ta'meer
Archive	محافظ خانہ	muhaafiz khaana
Archives	محافظ خانہ	muhaafiz khaana
Ardent	پرجوش	purjosh
Arduous	مشکل	mushkil

Are	ہیں	hayn
Area	رقبہ	raqba
Area	پھیلاؤ	phelao
Arena	میدان	maidan
Argue	بحث کرنا	behes karna
Argument	بحث	behes
argument noun	موقف	mauqif
Arid	خشک	khushk
Arise	جاگنا	jaagna
Ark	کشتی	kishti
Arm	بازو	baazoo
Arm	آستین	aasteen
armed adjective	مسلح	musallah
Armour	زرہ بکتر	zarah-baqtar
Armpit	بغل	baghal
Arms	ہتھیار	hathyaar
Army	سپاہ	sippah
Arnold noun; name	آرنلڈ	arnold

Aroma noun	مہک	mehek
Aromatic adjective	خوشبو دار	khushbudaar
Around	اطراف	atraaf
Arouse	بیدارکرنا	bedaar karna
Arraign	مجرمٹھہرانا	mujrim thheraana
Arrange	ترتیب دینا	tarteeb dena
Arrange	انتظام کرنا	intezaam karna
Arrangement	ترتیب	tarteeb
Array	ترتیب دینا	tarteeb dena
Arrear	بقایا	baqaaya
Arrest	گرفتار کرنا	giriftaar karna
Arrival	آمد	aamad
Arrive	آنا	aana
Arrive	پہنچنا	pohonchna
Arrogance	غرور	gharoor
Arrogant	مغرور	maghroor
Arrow	تیر	teer

Arsenal	اسلحہ	aslahaa
Arson	آگ لگانا	aag lagaana
Art	آرٹ	art
Art	ہنر	hunar
Art	پیشہ	pesha
Art	عیاری	ayyari
Artery	رگ	rag
Article noun; essay	مضمون	mazmoon
Article noun; item	اجزاء	ajzaa
Articulate	بولنا	bolnaa
Articulation	تلفظ	talaffuz
Artificial	نقلی	naqlee
Artillery	ارٹلری	artillery
Artisan noun	ہنرمند	hunar-mand
Artist	فنکار	fankaar
As	جیسا	jesa
As	مانند	maanind

Ascend	چڑھنا	charhna
Ascribe	منسوب کرنا	mansub karna
Ash	خاک	khaak
Ashamed	شرمندہ	sharminda
Ashes	راک	raakh
Ashore	ساحل پر	saahil par
Asia	ایشیا	asia
Aside	ایک طرف	aik taraf
Asif noun; male name	آصف	Asif
Ask	پوچھنا	poochhna
Ask	مانگنا	mangna
Asleep	سوتاہوا	sota huwa
Aslope	ڈھلوان	dhalwaan
Aspect	منظر	manzar
Asperity	ناہموار	naa-hamwaar
Asperse	عیب لگانا	aib lagaana
Asphalt	رال	raal
Aspirate	ہکارنا	hakaarna

aspiration Noun	امنگ	umang
Aspiration Noun	آرزو	aarzu
Aspire	آرزو کرنا	arzoo karna
Ass	گدھا	gadhha
Assail	چڑھائی کرنا	charhai karna
Assail	حملہ کرنا	hamlaa karna
Assassin	قاتل	qaatil
Assault	چڑھائی	charhaai
Assault	حملہ	hamlaa
Assay	آزمائش	azmaaish
Assemble	جمع کرنا	jamaa karna
Assembly	مجلس	majlis
Assent	منظور کرنا	manzoor karna
Assert	حق جتانا	haq jitaana
Assess	اندازہ لگانا	andaaza lagaana
Assets	اثاثہ	asaasa
Assign	مخصوص کرنا	makhsoos karnaa

Assign	منسوب کرنا	mansoob karna
Assigned	مخصوص	makhsoos
Assignment	سپردگی	sapurdgi
Assignment	کام	kaam
Assimilate	یکساں کرنا	yaksaan karna
Assist	مدد کرنا	madad karna
Assistance	مدد	madad
Assistant	مددگار	madadgaar
Associate	ساتھی	saathi
Association	انجمن	anjuman
Assort	ترتیب دینا	tarteeb dena
Assortment	ترتیب	tarteeb
Assuage	ہلکا کرنا	halkaa karna
Assume	فرض کرنا	farz karna
Assumption	اندازہ	andaaza
Assurance	یقین	yaqeen
Assure	یقین دلانا	yaqeen dilaana

Astern	پیچھے	pichay
Astonish	حیران ہونا	hairaan hona
Astonishment	حیرانی	hayraani
Astound	حیران کرنا	hairaan karna
Astray	گمراہ	gumraah
Astrology	علم نجوم	ilm-e-nujum
Astronomy	علم ہیئت	ilm-e-hai't
Astute	ہوشیار	hoshyaar
Asunder	علیحدہ علیحدہ	a'lehdaa a'lehdaa
Asylum	دارالامان	daar-al-aman
At	پر	par
At	کے	kay
At	سے	say
Ate	کھایا	khaaya
Atheism	دہریت	dah'reeyyat
Atheist	لامذہب	laa-mazhab
Athlete	کھلاڑی	khilaari

Athletic	ورزشی	warzishi
Athletics	ورزش	warzish
Atlantic	اوقیانوس	oqiyanus
Atlas	نقشہ	naqshaa
Atmosphere	کرہ ارض	kurra-e-arz
Atom	ایٹم	atom
Atom	جوہر	johar
Atomic	جوہری	johiri
Atrocity	ظلم	zulm
Attach	جوڑنا	jorna
Attachment	تعلق	taa'luq
Attack	حملہ	hamlaa
Attain	حاصل کرنا	hasil karna
Attempt	کوشش کرنا	koshish karna
Attend	شرکت کرنا	shirkat karna
Attendance	حاضری	haazri
Attention	دھیان	dihaan

Attentive	متوجہ	mutawwajay
Attest	تصدیق	tasdeeq
Attic	بالاخانہ	bala khana
Attire	لباس	libaas
Attitude	رویہ	ra'wayya
Attorney	وکیل	wakeel
Attract	کھینچنا	khenchnaa
Attractive	دلکش	dilkash
Attribute	صفت	sift
Attrition	ندامت	nadaamat
Auburn	بھورا	bhoora
Auction	نیلام	nilaam
Audacious	گستاخ	ghustaakh
Audacity	گستاخی	ghus'taakhi
Audible	قابل سماعت	qabil-e-samaa'at
Audience	سامعین	samaeen

Audio	آواز	awaaz
Audit	حساب دیکھنا	hisaab dekhna
Auger	برما	barma
Aught	چاہئے	chaahiay
August	اگست	august
Aunt noun; paternal uncles wife	چچی	chachi
Aunt noun; maternal aunt	خالہ	khaala
Aunt noun; paternal aunt	پھپی	phuppi
Aunt maternal uncles wife	ممانی	mumaani
Aunty noun	آنٹی	aunty
Aura	مہک	mehek
Auricle	باہری کان	baahiri kaan
Auspice	شگون	shagoon
Auspicious	مبارک	mubaarak
Austere	سادگی پسند	saadgi pasand
Austerity	سادگی	saadgi
Authentic	اصلی	asli
Authenticate	تصدیق کرنا	tasdeek karnaa

Authenticity	تصدیق	tasdeek
Author	مصنف	musannif
Authority	اختیار	ikhteyaar
Authority	حکومت	hakoomat
Authorization	اختیار	ikhte'yaar
Authorize	اجازت دینا	ijaazat dena
Autocrat	خود مختار بادشاہ	khud-mukhtar badshah
Automatic	خودکار	khudkaar
Automation	خود کاری	khud-kaari
Autumn	خزاں	khazaan
Auxiliary	مددگار	madadgaar
Avail	فائدہ اٹھانا	faaidaah uthaana
Available	دستیاب	dasteyaab
Available	میسر	muyassir
Avarice	لالچ	laalach
avatar noun	آو اتار	avatar
Avenge	بدلا لینا	badla layna

Avenue	سڑک	sarak
Average	درمیانہ	darmiyaana
Averse	مخالف	mukhaalif
Aversion	اختلاف	ikhtelaaf
Avert	ہٹانا	hataana
Avoid	بچنا	bachna
Avow	اقرار کرنا	iqraar karna
Await	انتظار کرنا	intezaar karna
Awake	بیدار	bedaar
Award	انعام	inaam
Aware	آگاہ	aagah
Away	دور	door
Awe	حیرانی	hayraani
Awesome	زبردست	zabardast
Awful	خوفناک	khofnaak
Awkward	بدنما	badnuma
Awning	سائبان	saibaan

Awry	ترچھا	tirchaa
Axe	کلہاڑی	kulhaari
Axis	دھرا	dehra
Axle	دھرا	dehra
AZEEM adjective	عظیم	azeem
Azure	آسمانی	aasmaani

B

Babble	بک بک کرنا	bak bak karna
Babe	بچہ	bacha
Baboon	لنگور	langoor
Baby	بے بی	baby
Baby	ننھا بچہ	nanna bachcha
Bachelor	کنوارہ	kunwaara
Back	پیٹھ	peeth
Back	پشت	pusht
Back	پیچھے	pechhe
Back	پچھلا	pichhla
Back	مدد کرنا	madad karna
Back	تائید کرنا	taeed karna
Backbite	غیبت کرنا	ghai'bat karna
Backbone	ریڑھ کی ہڈی	rirh ki hadhi
Background	پس منظر	pas-e-manzar
Backlog	جمع شدہ	jamaa shudaa

Backward	پیچھے	peecchay
bacteria noun	جراثیم	jeraseem
Bad	برا	bura
Badge	نشان	nishaan
Baffle	حیران کرنا	hairaan karna
Bag	تھیلا	thelaa
Baggage	سازوسامان	saz-o-samaan
Bagpipe	باجہ	baajaa
Bail	ضمانت	zamaanat
Bait	چارہ	chaara
Bake	بیک	bake
Baker	نان بائی	naanbai
Balance	توازن	tawaazun
Balcony	بالکنی	baalkani
Bald	گنجا	ganjaa
Bale	گٹھا	ghatta
Ball	بال	ball
Ball	گیند	gaind

Ball	گولا	gola
Balloon	غبارہ	ghubaara
Ballot	پوشیدہ رائے	poshida raa'ay
Ballroom	رقص گاہ	raqsgah gaah
Balm	مرہم	marham
Balmy	خشبودار	khushbudaar
Bamboo	بانس	baans
Ban	پابندی	paabandi
Banana	کیلا	kaylaa
Band	بینڈ	band
Band	گروہ	groh
Band	پٹی	patti
Band	پٹی باندھنا	patti bandhna
Band	جمع کرنا	jama karna
Bandage	مرہم پٹی	marham patti
Bandit	ڈاکو	daaku
Bane	زہر	zeher
Bang	دھماکہ	dhamaaka

Bangle	چوڑی	choorrhi
Banish	جلا وطن کرنا	jalaa watan karna
Banishment	جلا وطنی	jala watni
Bank	بینک	bank
Bank	کنارہ	kinara
Bank	پشتہ	pushta
Bank	بھروسا کرنا	bharosa karna
Bankrupt	دوالیہ	diwaalia
Bankruptcy	دوالہ	diwaala
Banner	جھنڈا	jhandha
Banquet	ضیافت	ziyaafat
Banter	مزاق	mazaaq
Banyan	برگد	bargad
Bar	سلاخ	salakh
Bar	رکاوٹ	rukaawat
Bar	کٹہرا	katehra
Bar	شراب خانہ	sharab khana
Bar	وکلاء کی جماعت	wukla ki jamat

Bar	روکنا	rokna
Barbarian	وحشی	wehshi
Barber	نائی	naai
Barber noun	حجام	hajjaam
Bare	ننگا	nanga
Bargain	سودا	soda
Barge	ناؤ	nao
Bark	بھونکنا	bhonkna
Bark	چھال	chhaal
barley noun; crop	جو	jo
Barren	بنجر	banjar
Barrier	رکاوٹ	rukaawat
Barrister	وکیل	wakeel
Barrow	ٹھیلا	thhela
Base	بنیاد	bunyad
Base	اساس	asaas
Base	القلی	alqali
Base	بنیاد رکھنا	bunyad rakhna

Base	اعتماد کرنا	etamaad karna
Baseless	بےبنیاد	be-bunyad
Basement	تہ خانہ	teh khana
Bash	مارنا	maarna
Basharat noun; name	بشارت	Basharat
Bashful	شرمیلا	sharmeela
Basic	بنیادی	bunyadi
Basic	القلی سے متعلق	alqali se mutalliq
Basin	طاس	taas
Basis	بنیاد	bunyaad
Bask	سیکنا	sayknaa
Basket	ٹوکری	tokri
bastard adjective	حرامی	haraami
Bat	بیٹ	bat
Bat	چمگادڑ	chimgaadar
Bat noun; stick used to play cricket and other games	بلا	balla
Batch	گھان	ghaan

Bate	کم کرنا	kam karnaa
Bath	غسل	ghusal
Bathroom	غسل خانہ	ghusal-khaana
Battalion	لشکر	lashkar
Batter	آمیزہ	aamayzaah
Battery	توپ خانہ	top khaana
Battle noun	جنگ	jang
Battlefield noun	میدان جنگ	maydaan-e-jang
Bawl	چلانا	chillaana
Be	ہونا	hona
Be	موجود ہونا	mojood hona
Be	زندہ رہنا	zinda rehna
Be	باقی رہنا	baqi rehna
Beach	ساحل	saahil
Beacon	مینارنور	minaar-e-noor
Bead	موتی	moti
Beak	چونچ	chonch
Beam noun; wooden	شہتیر	shehteer

Beam noun; light beam	کرن	kiran
Bean noun	لوبیا	lobiya
Bear	ریچھ	reechh
Bear	سہنا	sehna
Bear	برداشت کرنا	bardaasht karna
Bear	سنبھالنا	sambhalnaa
Beard	داڑھی	daarhi
Bearer	حامل	haamil
Bearing	جانب	jaanib
Bearish	مثالبھال	misaal-e-bhaalu
Beast	وحشی جانور	wehshi jaanvar
Beat	شکست دینا	shikast dena
Beat	مارنا	maarna
Beat	بجانا	bajaana
Beat	شکست	shikast
Beat	چوٹ	chot
Beat	دل کی دھڑکن	dil ki dharkan
Beat	مقررہ گشت	muqarrara gasht

Beautiful	خوبصورت	khoobsoorat
Beauty	حسن	husn
Beauty	خوبصورتی	khubsurti
Because	چونکہ	choonkay
Beckon	بلانا	bulaana
Become	ہوجانا	ho jaana
Bed	پلنگ	palang
Bed	بستر	bistar
Bed	کیاری	kiyaari
Bed	تہہ آب	tah-e-aab
Bed	بستر میں لٹانا	bistar mein litana
Bed verb; to make a landscaping bed	کیاری بنانا	kiyaari banana
Bedazzle	چمکنا	chamakna
Bedroom	کمرا	kamra
bedroom noun	سونے کا کمرا	sonay ka kamrah
Bee	شہد کی مکھی	shehed ki makhi
Beech	شفتالو	shaftaalu
Beef	گائے کاگوشت	gaa'ay ka gosht

Been	ہوا	huwa
Beer	شراب	sharaab
Beet	چوقندر	chukandar
Befall	نازل ہونا	naazil hona
Befit	پورا آنا	pura aana
Before	پہلے	pehlay
Before	پچھلا	pichhlaa
Before	سامنے	saamnay
Beforehand	پہلے سے	pehlay say
Befriend	سات دینا	saath dayna
Beg	بھیک مانگنا	bheek maangana
Beget	پیدا کرنا	peda karna
Beggar	فقیر	faqeer
Begin	شروع کرنا	shuroo karna
Begin	شروع ہونا	shuroo hona
Beginner	مبتدی	mubtadi
Beginning	ابتداء	ibtayda
Behalf	واسطے	wastay

Behave	پیش آنا	paysh aana
Behaviour	برتاؤ	bartaao
Behead	سرقلم کرنا	sar qalam karna
Behind	پیچھے	peechhay
Behind	پشت	pusht
Behold	لو	lo
Being	ہونا	hona
Being	مخلوق	makhluq
Belch	ڈکار	dakaar
Belief	ایمان	imaan
Believe	سمجھنا	samajhna
Believe	یقین کرنا	yaqeen karna
Believe	بھروسا کرنا	bharosa karna
Bell	گھنٹی	ghanti
Bell	گھنٹی باندھنا	ghanti baandhna
Belligerent	جنگ آور	jang aawar
Bellow	چیخنا	cheekhna
Belly	پیٹ	pait

Belong	تعلق	taa'luq
Beloved	پیارا	piyaara
Below	نیچے	neechay
Belt	بیلٹ	belt
Bench	تختہ	takhta
Bend	موڑ	morh
Beneath	تلے	talay
Benefactor	کریم	kareem
Beneficial	مفید	mufeed
Beneficiary noun; receiver	وصول کنندہ	wasool koninda
Benefit	فائدہ	faaidaa
Benevolence	کرم	karam
Benign	مہربان	meherbaan
Bent	موڑ	morh
Benumb	سن کرنا	sun karna
Bequeath	وسیحت کرنا	waseehat karna
Bequest	وقف	waqf
Bereave	محروم کرنا	mehroom karna

Berry	بیری	berry
Beseech	درخواست کرنا	darkhuaast karna
Beset	گھیر لینا	gher lena
Beside	پاس	paas
Besides	علاوہ	ilaawah
Besiege	گھیر لینا	gher lena
Best	بہترین	behtareen
Bestow	بخشنا	bakhshna
Bet	شرط	shart
Betray	دھوکا دینا	dhoka dena
Better	بہتر	behtar
Between	درمیان	darmiyan
Beverage	شربت	sharbat
Bewail	افسوس کرنا	afsos karna
Beware	ہوشیار	hoshyaar
Bewitch	جادو کرنا	jaadu karna
Beyond	اس پار	us paar
Bias	طرف داری	tarafdaari

Bible	انجیل	injeel
Bicker	جھگڑنا	jhagarna
Bicycle	بائسکل	bicycle
Bid	بولی لگانا	boli lagana
Bidding	فرمان	farmaan
Bide	رہنا	rehna
Big	بڑا	bara
Bill	نوٹ	note
Bill	چونچ	chonch
Billion	دس کھرب	das kharab
Billow	لہر	leher
Bin	ٹوکرا	tokara
Bind	باندھنا	baandhna
Bind noun; construction field	باندنا	bandhna
Binder	جلدساز	jild-saaz
Binding	جلد	jild
Binoculars	دوربین	durbeen
Biographer	تذکرہ نویس	tazkiraah navees

Biography	سرگزشت	sarguzisht
Biology	حیاتیات	hayaatiyaat
Birch	بید	bed
Bird	پرندہ	parinda
Bird noun; bird	پرندہ	parinda
Birth	پیدائش	paydaaish
Birthday	سالگرہ	saalgiraah
Biscuit	بسکٹ	biscuit
Bisect	نصف کرنا	nifs karna
Bit	ذرہ سا	zaraa saa
Bit	پرزہ	purzaa
Bit	ٹکڑا	tukrha
Bitch	کتیہ	kutiya
Bite	کاٹ	kaat
Bitter	کڑوا	karhwaa
Black	کالا	kala
Black	سیاہ	siah
Blacksmith	لوہار	lohaar

Bladder	مثانہ	masaanah
Blame	قصور	kasoor
Bland	نرم	naram
Blank	خالی	khaali
Blanket	کمبل	kambal
Blasphemy	کفر	kufr
Blast	دھماکہ	dhamaka
Blaze	آنچ	aanch
Bleach	اجالا	ujaala
Bleak	ویران	wiraan
Bleat	میمیانہ	memyaana
Bleed	خون نکالنا	khun nikaalna
Blend	ملاؤ	milaao
Bless	برکت دینا	barkat dena
Blessed	شاد	shaad
Blessing	رحمت	rehmat
Blight	آفت	aafat
Blind	نابینا	nabeena

Blindly	اندھا دھن	andhaa dhund
Blindness	نابینائی	naabinaai
Blink	جھپکنا	jhapakna
Bliss	فرحت	farhat
Blister	چھالا	chaala
Bloat	ابھرنا	ubharna
Block	بھاری لکڑی	bhari lakri
Block	بھاری پتھر	bhari patthar
Block	مکانوں کی قطار	makanon ki qatar
Block	روکنا	rokna
Block noun	حصہ	hissa
Blockade	روکاوٹ	rokaawat
blog noun	بلوگ	blog
Blood	خون	khoon
Bloodless	بےخون	baykhoon
Bloodshed	خون ریزی	khunrayzi
Bloodthirsty adjective	خون خوار	khoon khwaar
Bloody	بےرحم	bay-rehem

Bloom	شگفتہ	shagufta
Blossom	کھلنا	khilna
Blot	دھبا	dhabba
Blow	اڑانا	urhaana
Blow	پھونکنا	phoonkna
Blow	اڑنا	urhnaa
Blow	گھونسا	ghoonsaa
Blow	ضرب	zarb
Blow	صدمہ	sadma
Blow	بھک سے اڑا دینا	bhak say urhaa dena
Blue	نیلا	neela
Blue	آسمانی	aasmaani
Bluff	دھونس	dhons
Blunder	خطا	khataa
Blunt	کند	kund
Blur	دھندلا	dhundlaa
Blurt	کہ جانا	keh jaana

Blush	شرمندہ ہو جانا	sharminda ho jaanaa
Boar	جنگلی سؤر	jangli-suar
Board	تختہ	takhta
Board	میز	mez
Board	کھانا	khaana
Board	ارکان جماعت	arkaanay jamaat
Board	سوار ہونا	sawaar hona
Boast	شیخی	sheikhi
Boat	کشتی	kashti
Boat noun	سفینہ	Safeena
Boatman	ملاح	mullah
Bodice	کرتی	kurti
Body	جسم	jism
Body noun; organization	جماعت	jamaat
Bodyguard	محافظ	muhaafiz
Bog	دلدل	daldal
Bogus	جالی	jaali
Boil	ابلنا	ubalnaa

Bold	دلیر	dalayr
Bolt	دوڑنا	dorhna
Bolt	بجلی	bijli
Bomb	بم	bomb
Bombard	گولا باری	golaa-baari
Bonafide	صحیح	saheeh
Bond	معاہدہ	muaa'hida
Bone	ہڈی	haddi
Bonus	نفح	nafaah
Boob noun	چھاتی	chaati
Boobs noun	چھاتی	chhaati
Book	کتاب	kitab
Booklet	کتابچہ	kitaab-chaa
Bookmark	بک مارک	bookmark
boon noun; as in blessing	نعمت	namat
Boot	جوتا	jootaa
Booth	مقررہ جگہ	muqarrara jagaah
Border	کنارہ	kinaara

Bore	سراخ	suraakh
Bored	بیزار	bayzaar
Born	پیدا ہونا	peda hona
Borrow	قرض	qarz
Boss	مالک	maalik
Botany	علم نباتات	ilm-e-nabaataat
Both	دونوں	dono
Bother	فکرمند ہونا	fikarmand hona
Bottle	بوتل	bottle
Bottom	پیندہ	paynda
Bottom	تہہ	teh
Bottom	نچلا	nichlaa
Bough	ڈھال	dhhaal
Bought	خریدا ہوا	khareeda hua
Bounce	چھلانگ	chhalaang
Bound	محدود	mehdood
Boundary	صرحد	sarhad
Bounteous	کریم	kareem

Bounty	سخاوت	sakhaawat
Bouquet	گلدستہ	guldastaa
Bow	جھکنا	jhuknaa
Bowl	پیالا	piyaala
Box	ڈبہ	dabba
Box	صندوق	sandooq
Box	مکے مارنا	mukkay marnaa
Box noun	پٹارا	pitaaraa
Boy	لڑکا	larka
Brace	کسنا	kasnaa
Bracelet	چوڑی	churhi
Braid	لڑی	larhi
Brain noun	مغز	maghz
Brake noun	آلہء ضبط رفتار	Aala-e-Zabt-e-Raftaar
Branch	شاخ	shaakh
Branch	نسل	nasal
Branch	شاخ نکلنا	shaakh nikalna

Branch	شاخوں میں تقسیم ہونا	shaakhon mein taqseem hona
Brass	پیتل	peetal
Brave	دلیر	dalayr
Bravery	دلیری	dalayri
Bravo	واہ واہ	wah wah
Brawl	جھگڑنا	jhagarhna
Brawn	طاقت	taaqat
Breach	ناچاقی	naa-chaaqi
Bread noun	روٹی	roti
Bread noun; livelihood	روزی	rozi
Bread noun	نان	naan
bread noun; soft pita	چپاتی	chapaati
Breadth	چوڑائی	choraai
Break	ٹوٹنا	tootna
Break	توڑنا	torhna
Break	وقفہ	waqfa
Break	توڑپھوڑ	torh phorh

Break	شگاف	shigaaf
Breakfast	ناشتہ	naashta
Breast	چھاتی	chhaati
Breath	دم	dam
Breathe	سانس لینا	saans layna
Breathless	بےدم	bay-dam
Breed	نسل	nasal
Breeding	پرورش	parwarish
Breeze	نسیم	naseem
Brevity	اختصار	ikhtesaar
Brew	پیدا کرنا	payda karna
Bribe	رشوت	rishwat
Bribery	رشوت ستانی	rishwat sataani
Brick	اینٹ	eent
Bridal	بیاہ	biyaah
Bride	دلہن	dulhan
Bridegroom	دلہا	dulhaa
Bridge	پل	pul

Bridle	لگام دینا	lagaam dena
Brief	مختصر	mukhtasar
Bright	روشن	roshan
Bright	شوخ	shokh
Bright	ہشاش بشاش	hashaash bashaash
Brighten	روشن کرنا	roshan karna
Brilliance	چمک	chamak
Brilliant	منور	munawwar
Brim	کنارہ	kinaara
Bring	لانا	laana
Bring	پیش کرنا	paysh karna
Brink	کنارہ	kinaara
Brisk	پھرتیلا	phurteela
Brittle	نازک	naazuk
Broad	چوڑا	chorha
Broad	وسیع	waseeh
Broaden	چوڑا کرنا	chora karna
Broil	لڑائی	larhaai

Broke verb	توڑ دیا	torh diyaa
Broke	دیوالیہ	diwaalya
Broken adjective	ٹوٹا ہوا	tutaa hua
Bronze	کانسی	kaansi
Brood	اندیشا کرنا	andaysha karna
Brook	برداشت	bardaasht
Broom	جھاڑو	jhaarhu
Brother	بھائی	bhai
Brotherhood	بھائی چارہ	bhaai chaara
Brought	لایا	laaya
Brought	لایا گیا	laaya gya
Brown	بھورا	bhoora
Brown	خاکی	khaaki
Brown	بھوننا	bhoonna
Browse	چرنا	charna
Browse	دیکھنا	daykhna
Browser	دیکھنے والا	dekhnay waala
Bruise	چوٹ	chot

Brush	برش	brush
Brutality	بے رحمی	bay-rehmi
Brute	بے تمیز	bay-tameez
Bucket	بالٹی	baalti
Buckle	بکسوا	bakswaa
Bud	کلی	kali
Buddhism	بدھ مت	budh-mat
Buddhist	بدھ	budh
Buddy noun	یار	yar
Budge	ہٹانا	hataana
Buffalo	بھینس	bhens
Bug	کھٹمل	khatmal
Build	بنانا	banaana
Build	تعمیر کرنا	taameer karna
Builder	بنانے والا	banaanay waala
Building	تعمیر کرنا	taa'meer karnaa
Bulk	دھیر	ddhayr
Bulky	موٹا	motaa

Bull	سانڈ	saandh
Bullet	گولی	goli
Bullock	بیل	bayl
Bully	لڑاکا	larhaaka
Bump	اچھلنا	uchhalna
Bunch	گچھا	guchha
Bundle	گھٹڑی	ghattri
Bungalow	بنگلہ	bungalow
Burden	بوج	bojh
Bureaucrat	بیوروکریٹ	bureaucrat
Burglar	چور	chor
Burial	جنازہ	janaaza
Burly	بھاری	bhaarri
Burn	جلنا	jalna
Burn	جلانا	jalaana
Burn	چھالہ	chhaala
Burrow	بل	bil
Burst	پھوٹنا	phootnaa

Bury	دفن کرنا	dafn karna
Bus	بس	bus
Bus noun	بڑی مسافرگاڑی	Bari musaafar gaari
Bush	جھاڑی	jhaarri
Business	کاروبار	kaarobaar
Bustle	جلدی کرنا	jaldi karnaa
Busy	مصروف	masroof
Busy	مصروف ہونا	masroof hona
But	مگر	magar
But	صرف	sirf
But	علاوہ	ilaawa
But	بلکہ	balkay
Butcher	قصائی	qasaai
Butler	خانساماں	khaan-saamaan
Butter	مکھن	makkhan
Butterfly	تتلی	titly
buttock noun	چوتڑ	chotar
Button	بٹن	button

Buy	خریدنا	khareednaa
Buzz	بھنبھناہٹ	bhinbhinaahat
By	قریب	qareeb
By	سامنے	samnay
By	ساتھ	saath
Bye	خداحافظ	khuda-hafiz
Bye	الوداع	al-wida

C

Cab	ٹیکسی	taxi
Cabbage	گوبی	gobi
Cabin	کمرا	kamra
Cabinet	چھوٹی الماری	chhoti almaari
Cable	مضبوط رسا	mazboot rassa
Cable	کیبل	cable
Cackle	کڑکڑ	kur kur
Cafe	چائےخانا	chaay khaana
Cage	پنجرہ	pinjraa
Cake	کیک	cake
Calamity	آفت	aafat
Calculate	گنتی کرنا	ginti karna
Calculation	حساب	hisaab
Calendar	کلینڈر	calendar
Calf	بچھڑا	bachraa
Calibre	ذہانت	zahaanat

Caliph	خلیفہ	khalifa
Caliphate	خلافت	khilaafat
Call	چلانا	chillaanaa
Call	فون کرنا	phone karna
Call	آواز	aawaaz
Call	حکم	hukum
Call	بلاوہ	bulaawaa
Call	بلانا	bulaanaa
Calligraphy	خوش خطی	khushkhati
Callous	سخت	sakht
Calm	سکون	sakoon
Came	آیا	aayaa
Camel	اونٹ	oont
Camp	کیمپ	camp
Camp	خیمہ	khema
Campaign	معرکہ	maarka
Can	ممکن ہونا	mumkin hona

Can	ٹین کا ڈبہ	teen ka dabba
Canal	نہر	neher
Canary	کنیری	canary
Cancel	ترک کرنا	tark karnaa
Candid	مخلص	mukhlis
Candle	مومبتی	moam-batti
candy noun	مٹھائی	mittaai
Cane	چھڑی	chharhi
Canister	کنستر	canister
Cannon	توپ	toap
Canoe	ناؤ	naao
Canopy	چھتر	chattar
Cant verb	نہیں کر سکنا	nahee kar sakna
Canvas	کنوس	canvas
Cap	ٹوپی	topi
Capability	قابلیت	qaabliyat
Capable	قابل	qaabil
Capacious	کشادہ	kushaada

Capacity	گنجائش	gunjaaish
Capital	دار الحکومت	darul hukumat
Capital	سرمایہ	sarmaayaa
Capital	بڑا	barhaa
Capital	اہم	ehem
Capsicum noun	شملہ مرچ	shimlaa mirch
Capsize	الٹ جانا	ulat jaana
Capsule	گولیاں	golian
Captain	کپتان	captain
Captain	سربراہ	sarbaraah
Captivate	قید کرنا	qed karna
Captive	قیدی	qaidi
Captivity	قید	qaed
Capture	قبضہ	qabzaa
Car	کار	car
Car	گاڑی	gaari
Caravan	کاروان	caravan

Carbon	کوئلہ	koilaa
Carcass	ٹھٹھیری	thathayri
Card	کارڈ	card
Card	گتہ	gatta
Card	تاش	taash
cardamom Spice	الائچی	Illaichi
Cardinal	عظیم	azeem
Care	خیال کرنا	khayaal karnaa
Care	خیال	khayaal
Care	توجہ	tawajjo
Care	توجہ دینا	tawajjo dena
Care	نگرانی	nigraani
Care	نگرانی کرنا	nigraani karna
Career	طرز زندگی	tarz-e-zindagi
Careful	محتاط	muhtaat
Careless	لاپرواہ	laa-parwaah
Caress	لاڈ	laadh
Caretaker	نگراں	nigraan

Cargo	سامان	samaan
Carnage	خون ریزی	khunrayzi
Carnivorous	گوشت خور	gosht-khor
Carol	گیت	geet
Carp	عیب نکالنا	aib nikaalna
Carpenter	ترکھان	tarkhaan
Carpet	قالین	qaaleen
Carriage	گاڑی	gaari
Carrot	گاجر	gaajar
Carry	اٹھانا	oothaana
Carry	لے جانا	lay jaanaa
Carry	پہنچانا	pohanchaana
Cart	گاڑی	gaari
Carve	کھریتنا	khuraytnaa
Case	واقعہ	waaqia
Case	مقدمہ	muqaddima
Case	ڈبہ	dabba

Case	غلاف	ghilaaf
Casement	کھڑکی	khirhki
Cash	نقد	naqd
Cassette	کیسٹ	cassette
Caste Caste	ذات	zaat
Castle	قلعہ	qila
Casual	بے تکلف	bay-takalluf
Cat	بلی	billi
Catalogue	فہرست	fehrist
Catapult	غلیل	ghulayl
Cataract noun; eye disease due to increase in lens opacity	موتیا بند	motiya band
Catch	پکڑنا	pakarhna
Catch	قبضہ کرنا	qabzaa karnaa
Catch	شکار	shikaar
Catch	قبضہ	qabzaa
Cattle	مویشی	mowayshi
caught verb; past tense	پکڑا	pakraa

Cauldron	کڑھاؤ	karhaao
Cause	وجہ	wajaah
Cause	عمل میں لانا	amal mein laanaa
Caution	خیال	khiyaal
Cautious	محتاط	muhtaat
Cave	غار	ghaar
Cease	رکنا	ruknaa
Ceiling	چھت	chhat
Celebrate	جشن منانا	jashan manaana
Celebration	جشن	jashan
Cell	قید خانہ	qayd khaana
Cell	بیٹری	battery
Cemetery	قبرستان	qabristan
Cent	ڈالر کا سواں حصہ	dollar ka sowan hissa
Center	مرکز	markaz
Centre	درمیان	darmiyaan
Century	صدی	sadi

Cereal	اناج	anaaj
Ceremony	تقریب	taqreeb
Certain	یقینی	yaqeeni
Certain	کوئی	koee
Certain	کچھ	kuchh
Certainty	یقین	yaqeen
Chagrin	طیش دلانا	taysh dilaana
Chain	زنجیر	zanjeer
Chair	کرسی	kursi
Chair	میر مجلس	mir majlis
Chair	کرسی صدارت	kursi-e-sadaarat
Chair	صدارت کرنا	sadaarat karnaa
Chamber	کمرہ	kamraa
chameleon noun	گرگٹ	girgit
Champion	حامی	haami
Chance	موقع	moqaa
Chance	اتفاق	ittifaaq

Chance	امکان	imkaan
Chance	قسمت	qismat
Change	تبدیلی	tabdeelee
Change	بدلنا	badalnaa
Change	لباس بدلنا	libaas badalnaa
Chaos	بےترتیبی	bay-tarteebi
Chap	آدمی	aadmi
Character	کردار	kirdaar
Character	سیرت	seerat
Character	خاصیت	khaasiyat
Character	علامت	alaamat
Charge	قیمت	qeemat
Charge	حملہ	hamlaa
Charge	الزام	ilzaam
Charge	نگرانی	nigraanee
Charge	حملہ کرنا	hamlaa karnaa
Charge	مطالبہ کرنا	mutaalbaa karnaa

Charge	الزام لگانا	ilzaam lagaanaa
Charge	عہدہ	ohdaa
Charity	خیرات	khayraat
charming adjective	دلربا	dilruba
Chart	چارٹ	chart
Chart	نقشہ	naqshaa
Chart	نقشہ بنانا	naqshaa banaana
Chase	تعاقب	taa'qub
Chastise	سزا دینا	sazaa dayna
Chat	بات چیت	baat cheet
Chauffeur	ڈرائیور	driver
Cheap	سستا	sasta
Cheat	دھوکا دینا	dhoka dayna
Check	چیک	check
Check	روک	rok
Check	سدباب	sad-e-baab
Check	جائزہ لینا	jaizaa laynaa
Check	روکنا	roknaa

Cheek	گال	gaal
Cheek noun	رخسار	rokhsaar
Cheer	جی خوش کرنا	ji khush karna
Cheerful	خوش مزاج	khush-mizaaj
Cheese	پنیر	paneer
Chemistry	کیمیا	keemiya
Chess noun	شطرنج	Shattrannj
Chest	سینہ	seenaah
Chew	چبانا	chubaana
Chick	چوزہ	chooza
Chicken	مرغی	murghi
Chief	چیف	chief
Chief	سردار	sardaar
Chief	سربراہ	sarbaraah
Chief	خاص	khaas
Child	بچہ	bachcha
childhood noun	بچپن	bachpan

Children	بچے	bachchay
Children	اولاد	olaad
Chill	ٹھنڈ	thand
Chilli	لال مرچ	laal-mirch
Chilly	ٹھنڈا	thandaa
China	چین	cheen
Choice	پسند	pasand
Choke	دم گھٹنا	dam ghhutnaa
Choose	چننا	chunna
Choose	انتخاب کرنا	intikhaab karnaa
Chop	کاٹنا	kaatna
Chord	دھن	dhun
Christian	نصرانی	nasraani
Christianity	عیسائیت	isaayat
Christmas	کرسمس	christmas
Chuckle	ہنسنا	hansnaa
Chunk	بڑاٹکڑا	baraa tukraa
Church	گرجا	girjaa

Cigarette	سگرٹ	cigarette
cinnamon noun; spice	دارچینی	darcheeni
Circle	دائرہ	daairaa
Circle	احاطہ	ahaataa
Circle	حلقہ	halqaa
Circle	جماعت	jamaat
Circle	گھیر لینا	gher laynaa
Circle	گول گھومنا	gol ghoomnaa
Circumstance	حالات	haalaat
Circumstances	حالات	haalaat
Citizen	شہری	shehri
City	شہر	shehr
Claim	استحقاق	istehqaaq
Claim	حق جتانا	haq jataanaa
Claim	مطالبہ	mutaalbaa
Claim	مطالبہ کرنا	mutaalbaa karnaa
Clap	تالی	taali

Clash	ٹکراؤ	takraao
Class	کلاس	class
Class	جماعت	jamaat
Class	طبقہ	tabqaa
Class	درجہ	darjaa
Claw	پنجہ	panjaa
Clay	مٹی	mitti
Clean	صاف	saaf
Clean	صاف کرنا	saaf karnaa
Clean	صاف ستھرا	saaf suthraa
Clean	صفائی کرنا	safai karnaa
Clean	صفایا کرنا	safaayaa karnaa
Clean	ختم کرنا	khatam karnaa
Clean	بےداغ	bay-daagh
Clear	صاف شفاف	saaf shaffaaf
Clear	روشن	roshan
Clear	ظاہر	zaahir
Clear	یقینی	yaqeeni

Clever	چالاک	chaalaak
Climate	آب و ہوا	aab-o-hawaa
Climax	عروج	urooj
Climb	چڑھنا	charhnaa
Climb	سر کرنا	sar karnaa
Climb	چڑھائی	charhhai
Cling	چمٹنا	chamatna
Clinic	ہسپتال	hospital
Clip	کترنا	kutarna
Clock	گھڑی	gharee
Clock	گھنٹا	ghanta
Clone	ہم جنس	ham-jins
Close	بند کرنا	band karnaa
Close	بند	band
Close	قریب	qareeb
Cloth noun	کپڑا	kapra
Clothe	کپڑے پہننا	kaprhay pahennaa

Clothe	ڈھانپنا	dhaanpnaa
Clothes	لباس	libaas
Clothing noun	کپڑے	kapray
Cloud	بادل	baadal
Cloud	بادل چھانا	baadal chhaanaa
clove noun; herb spice	لونگ	laung
clown noun	مسخرہ	maskhara
Cluck	کٹ کٹ	kut kut
Clue	عقدہ	uqdaah
Clutch	جکڑنا	jakarnaa
Coach	گاڑی	gaari
Coal	کوئلہ	koylaa
Coarse	کھردرا	khurdura
Coast	ساحل	saahil
Coat	کوٹ	coat
Coat	پوست	post
Coat	سمور	samoor
Coat	تہہ	teh

Coat	تہہ چڑہانا	teh charhhaana
Cobbler	موچی	mochi
Cobweb	جالا	jaalaa
Cock	مرغا	murghaa
Coconut	ناریل	naariyal
Coffee	کافی	coffee
Coil	گولہ	golaa
Coin	سکہ	sikka
Coincide	ملنا	milnaa
Cold	سرد	sard
Cold	ٹھنڈ	thand
Cold	ٹھنڈا	thandaa
Cold	نزلہ زکام	nazlaa zukaam
Collapse	گرنا	girnaa
Collect	جمع کرنا	jamaa karna
Collect	وصول کرنا	wusool karnaa
Collect	اخذ کرنا	akhz karnaa

Collection	مجموعہ	majmuaa
College	کالج	college
Collide	ٹکرانا	takraana
Collision	ٹکراؤ	takraao
Color	رنگ	rang
Color	رنگ کرنا	rang karnaa
Colorless adjective	بےرنگ	bay-rang
Colour noun	رنگ	rang
Column	کالم	column
Column	ستون	sutoon
Comb	کنگھی	kangi
Combination	میل	mayl
Combine	ملانا	milaana
Come	آنا	aana
Comet	دمدار تارہ	dum-daar taara
Comfort	آرام	aaraam
coming verb	آنا	aana
Command	حکم دینا	hukum dayna

Comment	تبصرہ	tabsiraa
Committee noun	انجمن	anjuman
Common	عام	aam
Common	معمولی	maamoolee
Common	روزمرہ کا	rozmarrah kaa
Common	عوام سے متعلق	awaam se mutallaq
Communicate	رابطہ کرنا	raabtaa karnaa
Communication	رابطہ	raabtaa
Community	فرقہ	firqaa
Companion	ساتھی	saathi
Company	کمپنی	company
Company	محفل	mehfil
Company	گروہ	groh
Compare	موازنہ کرنا	mawaaznaa karnaa
Compassion noun	ہمدردی	hamdardi
Compassionate	ہمدرد	hamdard
Compel	زبردستی کرنا	zabardasti karnaa

Compete	مقابلہ کرنا	muqaabala karna
Competition	مقابلہ	muqaabala
Compile	جمع کرنا	jamaa karnaa
Complain	شکایت کرنا	shakaayat karnaa
Complaint	شکایت	shakaayat
Complete	مکمل	mukammal
Complete	پورا کرنا	pooraa karna
Complexion noun	چہرے کا رنگ	chehre ka rang
Compliance noun	تَکمیل حُکَم	takmil e hukum
Complicate	پیچیدہ کرنا	paycheeda karna
Complicate	مشکل کرنا	mushkil karnaa
Compliment	تاریف	taareef
Comprehension	سمجھ	samajh
comprehensive adjective	جامع	jaamah
Comprise	مشتمل	mushtamil
Comprising	مشتمل	mushtamil
Compulsion	زبردستی	zabardasti

Compulsory	لازم	laazim
Computer	کمپیوٹر	computer
Conceive	تصور کرنا	tasawwur karnaa
Concentrate	یکجا جمع کرنا	yakja jamaa karnaa
Concentrate	غور کرنا	ghor karnaa
Concept	تصور	tasawwur
Concern	سروکار	sarokaar
Concern	فکر	fikr
Concrete Adjective	ٹھوس حقیقی	Toss Haqeeqi
condemnation noun	مزمت	muzammat
Condition	حالت	haalat
Condition	کیفیت	kefiyat
Condition	شرط	shart
condolence verb	تعزیت	Tazeeat
Condom noun; contraception	کنڈوم	condom
Confess	اقرار کرنا	iqraar karnaa
confess verb	اعتراف کرنا	aitraaf karnaa

Confidence	بھروسا	bharosaa
Confident	بھروسا کرنے والا	bharosa karnay waala
Confidential	رازدار	raazdaar
confirm verb	تصدیق	tasdeeq
conflict noun	اختلاف	ikhtelaf
conflict noun	کشیدگی	kasheedgi
conflict noun	کشمکش	kashmakash
Confuse	الجھانا	uljhaana
Confusion	افرا تفری	afraa tafri
Congenial	ہم مزاج	ham-mizaaj
Congest	بھر جانا	bhar jaanaa
Congested	بھرا ہوا	bharaa huwa
Congestion	تنگی	tangi
Congratulate	مبارک باد کہنا	mubaarak-baad kehna
Congratulation	مبارک باد	mubarak-baad
Congratulations noun	مبارک	mubaarik
Connect	جوڑنا	jorhnaa

Connect	ملانا	milaana
Connection	رشتہ	rishtaa
Conquer	فتح کرنا	fataah karnaa
Conqueror	فاتح	faateh
Conquest	فتح	fataah
Conscience	ضمیر	zameer
Conscience	ایمان	imaan
Conscious	باخبر	baa-khabar
Conscious	آگاہ	aagaah
consent verb; to accept	منظور کرنا	manzoor karna
Consequence	سبب	sabab
Consequent	نتیجے میں	nateejay mein
Consequently	لہذا	lahaazaa
conservative adjective	قدامت پسند	qadamat pasand
Consider	غور کرنا	ghor karnaa
Consider	توجہ دینا	tawajjo dayna
Considerable	معقول	maa'qool

Considerably	کافی حد تک	kaafi had tak
Consideration	غور	ghor
Consist	مشتمل ہونا	mushtamil hona
Consistency	استحکام	istehkaam
Consistent	یکساں	yaksaan
console verb	تسلی دینا	tasalli dena
Consonant	مطابق	mutaabiq
Consonant	موافق	muafiq
Consonant	ہم آہنگ	ham aahang
Conspiracy	سازش	saazish
Conspirator	سازشی	saazishi
Conspire	سازش کرنا	saazish karna
constitution noun	دستور	dustoor
Construct	تعمیرکرنا	taa'meer karna
Construction	تعمیر	taa'meer
Consult	مشورہ کرنا	mashwaraa karnaa
Consultant	مشورہ گیر	mashwaraa-geer

Consume	خرچکرنا	kharch karnaa
Consumption	خرچ	kharch
Contact	رابطہ	raabtaa
Contain	شامل کرنا	shaamil karnaa
Contain	گھیرنا	ghayrnaa
Contain	ضبط کرنا	zabt karnaa
Contain	قابو پانا	qaaboo paana
Contemplate	غور کرنا	ghor karnaa
Contemporary	ہم عمر	ham-umar
contempt noun	ذلت	zillat
content adjective	قناعت پسند	kanaat pasand
Continent	بر اعظم	bar-e-aazam
Continent	پرہیز گار	perhez gaar
Continue	جاری رکھنا	jaaree rakhnaa
Continue	برقرار رکھنا	barqaraar rakhnaa
Contract	معاہدہ	muwaahida
Contribute	اعانت کرنا	iyaanat karnaa

Contribution	اعانت	iyaanat
Control	قابو	qaaboo
Control	اختیار	ikhtiyaar
controversial adjective	اختلافی	ikhtelaafi
convenience noun	سہولت	sahoolat
convenient adjective	آسان	asaan
Conversation	گفتگو	guftagoo
Convert Noun	نومذہب	nau mazhab
Convert Verb	تبدیل کرنا	tabdeel karna
convict verb	جرم ثابت کَرنا	jurm sabit karna
Cook	باورچی	baawarchi
Cooking verb; female	پکا رھی ہے	paka rahi hey
Cooking verb; male	پکا رھا ہے	paka raha hey
Cool	ٹھنڈا	thandaa
Cool	سرد	sard
Copper	تانبا	taanba

Copy	کاپی	copy
Copy	نقل	naqal
Copy	نقل اتارنا	naqal ootaarna
Coriander	دھنیا	dhaniyaa
Corn	دانہ	daanaa
Corn	مکئ	makai
Corner	کونا	kona
Corner	گوشہ	gosha
Correct	ٹھیک کرنا	theek karna
Correct	اصلاح کرنا	islaah karna
Correct	صحیح	saheeh
correspondent noun	نامہ نگار	naamah nigaar
Corrupt	بد اخلاق	bad-ikhlaaq
Corruption	بد عملی	bad-amli
Cost	قیمت	qeemat
Cost	خرچ	kharch
Cost	لاگت	laagat

Cost	خرچ ہونا	kharch hona
Cottage	کوٹھری	kothari
Cotton	کپاس	kapaas
Cotton	روئی	rooee
Cotton	کاٹن	cotton
Cough	کھانسی	khaansi
Could	سکتا	saktaa
Count	شمار	shumaar
Count	گنتی	ginti
Count	گننا	ginna
Count	حساب کرنا	hisaab karna
Country	ملک	mulk
Country noun	وطن	watan
couple noun	جوڑا	Jora
Courage	بہادری	bahaaduri
Course	راستہ	raasta
Course	کورس	course

court noun	عدالت	adaalat
Courtesan noun	طوائف	tawaaif
Courtyard	صحن	sehen
Cousin	بھائی	bhaai
Cover	ڈھانکنا	dhaankna
Cover	ڈھکن	dhakkan
Cover	غلاف	ghilaaf
Cover	پناہ	panaah
Cow	گائے	gaae
Coward	بزدل	buzdil
Cower	خوف سے جھکنا	khof say jhukna
crab noun	کیکڑا	kekra
Crack	شگاف	shagaaf
Craftsman	کاریگر	kaarigar
Crafty	چالباز	chaalbaaz
Crap noun; slang	بیکار	baykaar
Crash	تباہی	tabaahi

Crawl	رینگنا	reengnaa
Craze	پاگل پن	paagal-pan
Crazy	پاگل	paagal
Crease	شکن	shikan
Crease	سلوٹ	silwat
Create	پیدا کرنا	pedaa karna
Create	بنانا	banana
Creation	تخلیق	takhleeq
Creator	خالق	khaaliq
Creature	مخلوق	makhlooq
credit contraction	کسی بات کا سہرا ملنا	kisi bat ka sahra milna
credit noun	پیسہ	pesah
Creek	ندی	naddi
creep verb; to proceed slowly	رینگنا	reengna
Crescent	ہلال	hilaal
cricket noun; a sport	کرکٹ	cricket
Crime	جرم	jurm

Criminal	مجرم	mujrim
Criticism noun	تنقید	Tanqeed
criticize verb	تنقید کرنا	tanqid karna
Crook	بدمعاش	badmaash
Crooked	ٹیڑھا	tayrhaa
Crop	فصل	fasal
Crop	فصل کاٹنا	fasal kaatna
Cross	صلیب	saleeb
Cross	ترچھا	tirchha
Cross	کاٹنا	kaatna
Cross	ناراض	naraaz
Crouch	بیٹھ جانا	bayth jaana
Crow	کوا	kaawwa
Crowd	بھیڑ	bheerh
Crowd	مجمع	majmaa
Crown	تاج	taaj
Crucial adjective	بہت اہم	Bhut Aham

Cruel	ظالم	zaalim
Crumble	چورا کرنا	chura karna
Crumple	چڑ مڑ کرنا	churmur karnaa
Crush	پیسنا	peesna
Cry	رونا	rona
Cry	چیخنا	cheekhna
Cry	پکارنا	pukaarna
Cry	چیخ	cheekh
Cucumber noun; vegetable	کھیرا	kheera
Cuddle	گلے لگانا	galay lagaana
Culprit	مجرم	mujrim
Culture	تہذیب	tehzeeb
cumin noun; food	ذیرہ	zeera
Cunning	چالاک	chaalaak
Cup	پیالا	piyaalaa
Cupboard	الماری	almaari
Cure	علاج	ilaaj

Curiosity	تجسس	tajassus
curious adjective	مشتاق	mushtaaq
Current	موجودہ	mojoodaa
Current	لہر	leher
curriculum noun	نصابی کتابیں	nisabi kitabain
Curry	سالن	saalan
curse noun	بد دعا	bad dua
Curtain	پردہ	pardaa
Cushion	تکیہ	takiyaa
custody noun	حراست	hiraasat
Custom	رواج	rawaaj
Customer	گاہک	gaahak
Cut	کاٹنا	kaatnaa
Cut	زخم	zakham
Cute	پیارا	piyaara
Cute	پیاری	piyaari
Cyber	خیالی	khiyaali

D

Dab	نرمی سے لگانا	narmi say lagaana
Dacoit	ڈاکو	daaku
Dad	ابو	abbu
Daddy noun	ڈیڈی	abba
Daft	بے وقوف	baywaqoof
Dagger	خنجر	khanjar
Daily	روزانہ	rozaana
Dais	چبوترا	chabootaraa
Dam	بند	band
Damage	نقصان	nuqsaan
Damn	لعنت	laanat
Damnable	قابلملامت	qaabil malaamat
Damp	گیلا	geela
Dampness	نمی	nami
Dance	رقص	raqs
Dance	ناچنا	naachnaa

Danger	خطرہ	khatraa
Dangerous	خطرناک	khatarnaak
Dangle	لٹکانا	latkaana
Dank	گیلا	geela
Dare	دلیری	dalayree
Daring	بہادر	bahadur
Dark	تاریک	taareek
Dark	اندھیرا	andhayraa
Darling	پیارا	piyaara
Darn	مرمت کرنا	murammat karna
Dash	دوڑنا	dornaa
Data	اعداد و شمار	a'daad-o-shumaar
Database	ڈیٹابیس	database
Date	تاریخ	taareekh
Date	کھجور	khajoor
Daughter	بیٹی	bayti
Dawn	فجر	fajr

Day	دن	din
Daze	گھبرانا	ghabraana
Dead	مردہ	murdaa
Deaf	بہرہ	behra
Deal	کاروبار	karobaar karnaa
Dear	پیارا	piyaara
Dear	مہنگا	mehengaa
Dear	عزیز	azeez
Death	موت	mot
Debt	قرض	qarz
Decay	سڑنا	sarhnaa
deceased noun	مرحوم	marhoom
Deceit	دھوکا دینا	dhoka dayna
Deceive verb	دھوکا دینا	Dhoka dena
December	دسمبر	december
decent adjective	شایستہ	shaaista
decent adjective; male	اچھا	achha

decent adjective; female	اچھی	achhi
Decide	فیصلہ کرنا	fayslaa karnaa
Decimal	اعشاریہ	aashariya
Decimal	دسواں	daswaan
Decision	فیصلہ	faysalaa
Declare	اعلان کرنا	ilaan karnaa
Decline	زوال	zawaal
Decorate	سجانا	sajaana
Decrease	کم کرنا	kam karnaa
Dedicate	نظرکرنا	nazar karnaa
Dedication	نذر نیاز	nazar niyaaz
Deed	کرتوت	kartoot
Deem	سمجھنا	samajhnaa
Deep	گہرا	gehraa
Deer	ہرن	hiran
Defeat	ہرانا	haraana
Defend	حفاظت کرنا	hifaazat karna

Definite	حتمی	hatmi
Defy	انکار کرنا	inkaar karna
Degree	درجہ	darjaa
Degree	سند	sanad
Delay	دیر	dayr
delay verb	ملتوی کرنا	multawi karna
Delete	مٹانا	mitaanaa
Delicate	نازک	naazuk
Delicious	لذیذ	lazeez
Delight	خوشی	khushi
Deliver	پہنچانا	pohanchaana
Delude	بہکانا	behkaana
Deluge	سیلاب	sailaab
Delusion	فریب	farayb
Demand	مطالبہ	mutaalba
democracy noun	جمہوریت	jamhuriat
Demographic noun	ڈیموگرافک	Demographic

Demolish	گرانا	giraana
Demonstrate	ظاہر کرنا	zaahir karna
Demonstration	مظاہرہ	muzaahira
denounce verb	مزمت	muzammat
Dentist	دندان ساز	dandan-saaz
Deny	انکار کرنا	inkaar karnaa
Depart	رخصت ہونا	rukhsat hona
Departure	روانگی	rawaangi
Depend	بھروسا کرنا	bharosaa karnaa
Depend	انحصار کرنا	inhisaar karnaa
deposit noun	امانت	amaanat
Depreciate	گھٹنا	ghatna
Depreciation	تحقیر	tehqeer
Depress	اداس ہونا	udaas hona
Depression	افسردگی	afsurdagi
Depth	گہرائی	gehraai
Deride	مزاق اڑانا	mazaaq urhaana

Descend	اترنا	utaarna
Describe	بیان کرنا	beyaan karnaa
Description	وضاحت	wazaahat
Desert	صحرا	sehraa
Desert	چھوڑ دینا	chhorh dena
Deserted adjective; no sign of human	ویرانہ	veeraana
Deserve	حقدار ہونا	haqdaar hona
Design	ڈیزائن	design
Design	نمونہ	namoonaa
Design	نقشہ	naqshaa
Design	نقشہ بنانا	naqshaa banaanaa
Design	ایجاد کرنا	ijaad karnaa
Design	منصوبہ بنانا	mansooba banaanaa
Designation noun	متعین	mutayyen
Desire	خواہش	khoaahish
Despair	مایوسی	maayoosi

Desperate adjective; without caution	بے تامل	bay taamil
Despise	ناپسند کرنا	naa-pasand karna
despite preposition	باوجود اس کے	baawajood is ke
Destination	منزل	manzil
Destine	مقرر کرنا	muqarrar karna
Destiny	تقدیر	taqdir
Destroy	تباہ کرنا	tabaah karna
Destruction	تباہی	tabaahi
Detail	تفصیل	tafseel
Detective	سراغ رساں	suraagh rasaan
Determine	اندازہ لگانا	andaaza lagaana
Determine	فیصلہ کرنا	feslaa karnaa
Detest	نفرت کرنا	nafrat karna
Develop	ترقی کرنا	taraqqi karnaa
Develop	تیار کرنا	taiyaar karnaa
Develop	نشوونما پانا	nasho-nooma paanaa

Development noun	ترقي	Taraqqi
Deviate	پھرنا	phirnaa
Deviate verb	انہراف کرنا	Inheraaf karna
Deviation	تجاوز	tajaawuz
Device	آلہ	aala
Devil noun	ابلیس	iblees
Devotion	لگاؤ	lagaao
Dew	شبنم	shabnam
Dew noun	شبنم	shabnam
Diagnose	تشخیص کرنا	tashkhees karna
Dialect	بولی	boli
Diamond	ہیرا	heera
Diamond noun	الماس	almaas
dick noun; obscene term for penis	مردانہ عضو تناسل	mardana uzu-i-tanasul
Dictate	حکم دینا	hukam dena
Dictator	آمر	aamer
Dictionary	لغت	lughat

Did	کیا	kiyaa
Did	کرلیا	kar liyaa
Die	مرنا	marnaa
Die	ہلاک ہونا	halaak honaa
Died	فوت ہوا	fot huaa
Diet	خوراک	khoraak
Differ	اختلاف کرنا	ikhtilaaf karnaa
Differ	مختلف ہونا	mukhtalif honaa
Difference	فرق	farq
Different	مختلف	mukhtalif
Difficult	مشکل	mushkil
difficult adjective	کشیدہ	kasheedah
difficulty noun	دشواری	dushwari
Dig	کھودنا	khodna
Digest	ہضم کرنا	hazam karna
digestion noun	ہاضمہ	haazma
Digital	ڈجٹل	digital

Dignity	عظمت	azmat
Dilatory	سست	sust
Dim	مدہم	mudham
Dinner	کھانا	khaana
Dip	ڈبونا	dabonaa
Direct	سیدھا	seedhaa
Direct	راستہ سمجھانا	raasta samjhaana
Direct	براہ راست	barah-e-raast
Direction	سمت	simt
Dirt	گرد	gard
Dirty	میلا	mela
Disagree	اختلاف کرنا	ikhtaylaaf karnaa
Disagreement	اختلاف	ikhtaylaaf
Disappear	غائب ہونا	ghaaib hona
Disappoint	ناامید ہونا	naa-umeed hona
Disaster	تباہی	tabaahi
Disciple	مرید	mureed

discipline noun	تنظیم	tanzeem
Discourage	حوصلہ شکنی کرنا	hosla shakni karna
Discourse	اظہارخیال	izhaar-e-khiyaal
Discover	دریافت کرنا	daryaaft karna
Discovery	دریافت	daryaaft
discrepancy noun	اختلاف	ikhtilaf
Discuss	گفتگو کرنا	guftugoo karnaa
Discuss	بات چیت کرنا	baat cheet karnaa
Disease	بیماری	baymaari
Disgrace	بے عزتی	bay-izzati
Disguise	بھیس بدلنا	bhays badalna
Dishonest	بے ایمان	bay-imaan
Dishonesty	بے ایمانی	bay-imaani
Dislike	ناپسند کرنا	naa-pasand karna
Dismiss	رخصت کرنا	rukhsat karna
Display	دکھانا	dikhaana

Dispute verb d	متنازع	mutanaaza
Dissect	چاک کرنا	chaak karna
Dissolve	حل کرنا	hal karna
Distance	فاصلہ	faasila
Distant	دور	dur
Distant	فاصلے پر	faslay par
Distinct	منفرد	munfarid
Distress	پریشانی	parayshaani
Distribute	تقسیم کرنا	taqseem karnaa
Distribution	تقسیم	taqseem
Disturb	الجھن میں ڈالنا	uljhan mein daalna
Disturbance	خلل	khalal
Ditch	گڑھا	garhaa
Dive	غوطہ	ghota
Diverse adjective	رنگا رنگ	Ranga Rang
Divide	توڑنا	torhnaa
Divide	تقسیم کرنا	taqseem karnaa

Divide	حصے کرنا	hissay karnaa
divine adjective; exceptional	عمدہ	umda
Division	تقسیم	taqseem
Divorce	طلاق	talaaq
Dizzy	چکر آنا	chakkar aana
Do	کرنا	karnaa
Do	سرانجام دینا	sar anjaam dena
Doctor	ڈاکٹر	doctor
Doctrine	درس	dars
document noun	دستاویز	dustawez
Dodge	دھوکا دینا	dhoka dayna
Does	کرتا	kartaa
Does	کرتی	karti
Dog	کتا	kutta
Doing	کرنا	karna
Doll	گڑیا	gurhyaa
Dollar	ڈالر	dollar

Domain	علاقہ	ilaaqa
Dome	گنبد	gunbad
domestic adjective	گھریلو	ghareloo
Don't	نہیں کرو	naheen karo
Donate	عطیہ دینا	atiyyaa dena
Donation	عطیہ	atiyya
Done	ہوگیا	ho gayaa
Done	کرلیا	kar liyaa
Donkey	گدھا	gadha
dont contraction	مت	mat
Door	دروازہ	darwaazaa
Dose	خوراک	khoraak
Double	دوگنا	dugnaa
Double	دوگنا کرنا	dugnaa karnaa
Doubt	شک کرنا	shak karna
Doubtful	مشکوک	mashkuk
Down	نیچے	neechay

Down	نچلا	nichlaa
Down	اتارنا	utaarnaa
Down	اداس	udaas
Down	بیمار	bimaar
Download noun	اتارنا	utaarna
Downward	نچھلی جانب	nichhli jaanib
Doze	نیند	neend
Dozen	درجن	darjan
Drag	گھسیٹنا	ghaseetna
Drain	پانی کا نکاس	paani kaa nikaas
Draw	کھینچنا	khenchnaa
Dread	خوف	khof
Dreadful	خوفناک	khofnaak
Dream	خواب	khaab
Dream	خواب دیکھنا	khaab dekhnaa
Drench	بھیگنا	bheegna
Dress	لباس	libaas
Dress	لباس پہننا	libaas pehennaa

Dress	سجانا	sajaana
Dress	مرہم پٹی کرنا	marham patti karnaa
Drift	بہہ جانا	beh jaana
Drill	سوراخ کرنا	suraakh karna
Drink	پینا	peena
Drink	مشروب	mashroob
Drip	ٹپکنا	tapakna
Drive	چلانا	chalaanaa
Drizzle	بونداباندی	bundaa baandi
Droop	لٹکنا	latakna
Drop	بوند	boond
Drop	گرانا	giraanaa
Drop	گرنا	girnaa
Drought	قحط	qeht
Drown	ڈوبنا	doobna
Drowsiness	اونگ	oong
Drowsy	نیند میں	neend mein

Drum	ڈھول	dhol
Dry	خشک	khushk
Dry	سکھانا	sukhaanaa
Duck	بطخ	batakh
dude interjection	یار	yaar
Due	متوقع	mutawakko
Dull	غیر دلچسپ	ghayr dilchasp
Dumb	گونگا	gunga
Dump	گرا دینا	giraa dayna
Dungeon	قیدخانہ	qayd khaana
durability noun	پائیداری	paaidaari
durable adjective	پائیدار	paaidaar
During	دوران	doraan
Dust	گرد	gard
Duty	فرض	farz
Dwarf	بونا	bonaa
Dwell	بسنا	basnaa
Dweller	مقیم	muqeem

Dye	رنگ	rang
Dynamic	حرکت کرتی	harkat karti

E

Each	ہر ایک	her aik
Eager	بے قرار	bay qaraar
Eagle	عقاب	uqaab
Eample	مثال	misaal
Ear	کان	kaan
Ear	اناج کی بالی	anaaj kee baalee
Early	سویرے	sawayray
Early	جلدی	jaldi
Early	ابتدائ	ibtidaaee
Earn	کمانا	kamaana
Earnest	مشتاق	mushtaaq
Earning	کمائی	kamaai
Earring	بالی	baali
Earth	زمین	zameen
Earth	کرہ ارض	kurra-e-arz
Earth	خاک	khaak
Earth	زمین میں دبانا	zameen mein dabaanaa

Earthquake	زلزلہ	zalzala
Ease	آسانی	aasaani
Ease	آرام پہنچانا	aaram pohnchaana
Ease	نرمی کرنا	narmee karna
Ease noun	سہولت	sahoolat
Easily	آسانی سے	aasaani say
East	مشرق	mashriq
Eastern	مشرقی	mashraqi
Easy	آسان	aasaan
Eat	کھانا	khana
Eating verb; female	کھا رہی	kha rahi
Eating verb; male	کھا رہا	kha raha
Eccentric	بے مرکز	bay markaz
Echo	گونج	goonj
Eclipse	گرہن	girhan
Economic	اقتصادی	iqtesaadi
Economical	کفایت شعار	kafaayat shiyaar
Economics	اقتصادیات	iqtesaadiyaat
Economist	ماہر اقتصادیات	maahir-e-iqtesaadiyaat

Economize	کفایت شعاری کرنا	kafaatyat shiyaari karna
Economy	کفایت	kafaayet
Ecstasy	ازحدخوشی	az-had khushi
Edge	کنارا	kinaara
Edible	کھانے کے قابل	khaanay kay qabil
Educate	سکھانا	sikhaana
Education	تعلیم	taaleem
Effect	اثر	asar
Effect	اثر کرنا	asar karna
Effect	اثر ہونا	asar hona
Effective	موئثر	mo'assar
Effort	کوشش	koshish
Egg	انڈا	andaa
Ego noun	انا	ana
Egypt	مصر	misr
eid noun; muslim holiday	عید	eid
Eight	آٹھ	aath
Eighteen	اٹھارہ	athaara
Eighty	اسی	assi

Either	کوئ بھی	koee bhee
Elbow	کہنی	kohni
Elder	بزرگ	bazurg
Elect	انتخاب کرنا	intekhaab karna
Election	انتخاب	intekhaab
Electric	برقی	barqee
Electric	بجلی سے متعلق	bijlee se mutallaq
Electricity	بجلی	bijli
Element	عنصر	ansar
Elementary	ابتدائی	ibtaydaai
Elephant	ہاتھی	haathi
Eleven	گیارہ	giyaara
Elicit	نکالنا	nikaalna
eligible adjective	لائق	laiq
Eliminate	خارج کرنا	khaarij karna
Elope verb	آشنا کے ساتھ فرار ہونا	Aashna ke saath faraar hona
Else	ورنہ	warnaa
Else	کوئ اور	koee aur
Else	علاوہ	ilaawa

Email	ای میل	email
Emancipate	آزاد کرنا	aazaad karna
Emancipation	آزادی	aazaadi
Embarrass	شرمندہ کرنا	sharminda karna
Embarrassment	شرمندہ	sharminda
Embrace	گلے ملنا	galay milna
Emerge	نکلنا	nikaalna
Emigrate	ہجرت کرنا	hijrat karna
emotional adjective	جذباتی	jazbaati
emotions noun	جذبات	jazbaat
Emperor	شہنشاہ	Shehen-shaah
Emphasize verb	تاکید کرنا	taqeed karna
Empire	سلطنت	sultanate
Employ	ملازمت دینا	mulaazimat dayna
Employment	ملازمت	mulaazimat
Empty	خالی	khaali
enable verb	قابل بنانا	qabil banana
Encourage	حوصلہ بڑھانا	hosla barhaana
encyclopedia noun	انسکلوپیدیا	encyclopedia
End	انجام	anjaam

End	اختتام	ikhtitaam
End	آخری حصہ	aakhree hissa
Endeavour	جدوجہد	jid-o-jehed
Endorse	تصدیق کرنا	tasdeeq karna
Enemy	دشمن	dushman
Energetic	جوشیلہ	josheela
Energy	توانائ	tawanaai
Engage verb; to involve someone	مشغول کرنا	mashghool karna
Engine	انجن	engine
England	انگلستان	england
English	انگریزی	english
Engrave	کھودنا	khodna
Enjoy	لطف اٹھانا	lutf utaana
Enjoyment	لطف	lutf
Enormous	بہت بڑا	bohat baraa
Enough	کافی	kaafee
Enough	بہت	bohot
Enough	ضرورت کا	zaroorat kaa
Enter	داخل ہونا	daakhil hona

Enter	داخل کرنا	daakhil karna
Entertain	خاطر کرنا	khaatir karna
Entertainment	خاطر مدارت	khaatir madaarat
Enthusiasm	جوش	josh
enthusiasm noun	جستجو	justujoo
Entire	پورا	poora
Entrance	داخلہ	daakhla
Entry	داخلہ	daakhila
Envelop	لفافہ	lifaafa
Environment	ماحول	maahol
Envy	حسد کرنا	hasad karna
Equal	برابر	baraabar
Equal	مساوی	masaawee
Equal	برابر کرنا	baraabar karna
Equality	مساوات	masaawaat
Equate	برابر کرنا	baraabar karna
Equate	برابر ہونا	baraabar hona
Equipment	سامان	saamaan
Equivalent	متبادل	mutabaadil

Equivalent	جیسا	jesaa
Erase	مٹانا	mitaana
Erect	کھڑا کرنا	kharaa karna
Errand	پیغام	payghaam
Error	غلطی	ghalti
Escape	فرار ہونا	faraar hona
Especially	خاص طور پر	khaas tor per
Espionage	جاسوسی	jaasoosi
Essence	عطر	atar
Essential	لازمی	laazmi
establish verb	قائم کرنا	qaaim karnaa
Esteem	احترام	ayhtayraam
Estimate	انداذہ	andaaza
Eternal	پایدار	paaidaar
Eternity	ہمیشگی	hamayshgi
Ethics noun	احلاقیات	ilm al-ikhlaqiat kay usool
Evaluate	اندازہ لگانا	andaaza lagana
Eve	شام	shaam
Even	جفت عدد	juft adad
Even	اگرچہ	agarcheh

Even	ہموار	hamwaar
Even	برابر	baraabar
Evening	شام	shaam
Event	واقعہ	waaqia
Event	واردات	waardaat
Event	تقریب	taqreeb
Eventually	آخرکار	aakhir kaar
Ever	ہمیشہ	hameshaa
Ever	کسی وقت	kisi waqt
Evergreen	سدابہار	sadaa-bahaar
Every	سارا	sara
Every	ہر ایک	her aik
Everybody	ہرکوئی	har koi
everyday noun	روز	roz
Everything	ہرچیز	har cheez
Everywhere	ہرجگہ	har jagaah
evidence noun	صراحت	sarahat
Evil	برائی	buraai
Evolution noun	ارتقاء	irteqa
Exact	قطعی	qataee

Exact	برمحل	bar mahal
Exaggerate	بڑھا چڑھا کر	barhaa charhaa kar
Exalt	بلند کرنا	buland karna
Exam	امتحان	imtehaan
Examination	امتحان	imtehaan
Examine	معائنہ کرنا	muaa'inaa karna
Example	مثال	misaal
Exceed	تجاوز کرنا	tajawwuz karna
Excellent	بہترین	behtareen
Except	سوائے	siwae
Excess	ذیادتی	ziyaadati
Exchange	تبدیل کرنا	tabdeel karna
Excite	اکسانا	uksaana
Excite	جوش دلانا	josh dilaana
Excited	جوشیلا	josheelaa
Excitement	خوشی	khushi
Exclude	نکالنا	nikaalna
Exclusive	مخصوص	makhsoos
Excursion	تفریح	tafreeh

Excuse	معزرت	maa'zarat
Execute	قتل کرنا	qatal karna
Execute	انجام دینا	anjaam dayna
Exercise	مشق کرنا	mashq karna
Exercise	ورزش کرنا	warzish karna
Exercise	نافذ کرنا	naafiz karna
Exercise	مشق	mashq
Exercise	ورزش	warzish
Exhaust	تھک جانا	thak jaana
Exhibit	دکھانا	dikhaana
Exhibition	نمائش	numaaish
Exile	جلاوطن	jalaa-watan
Exist	ہونا	hona
Existance	وجود	wajood
existing adjective	موجودۂ	mojuda
Exit	نکلنےکاراستہ	nikalnay kaa raasta
Exorbitant	حد درجہ	had-darjaa
Expand	پھیلنا	phaylna
Expect	امید کرنا	ummeed karna
Expect	توقع کرنا	tawaqqo karna

Expectation noun	امید	umeed
Expedition	مہم	muhim
Expensive	مہنگا	mahengaa
Experience	تجربہ	tajarba
Experience	آزمائش	aazmaaish
Experienced	تجربہ کار	tajarbaa-kaar
Experiment	تجربہ	tajarba
Experiment	تجربہ کرنا	tajarbaa karna
Expert	ماہر	maahir
Explain	واضح کرنا	waazay karna
Explanation	تشریح	tashreeh
Explicit	واضح	waazeh
Explicitly	واضح تور پر	waazeh tor par
Exploration	کھوج	khoj
Explore	کھوج لگانا	khoj lagaana
Explosion	دھماکہ	dhamaaka
export verb	برآمد کرنا	baraamad
Express	فوری	fori
Express	ظاہر کرنا	zahir karna

Expression noun	اظہار	Izhar
extend verb	بڑھانا	berhana
Extension	پھیلاؤ	phaylaao
Extent	حد	had
External adjective	بیرونی	Bayrooni
Extra	اضافی	izaafi
extradition noun	حوالگی	havaalgi
Extraordinary	غیرمعمولی	ghayr-maa'mooli
Extreme	انتہا	intayhaa
Extremist	انتہا پسند	intayhaa pasand
Eye	آنکھ	aankh
Eye	دیکھنا	dekhna
Eyes noun	آنکھیں	aankhaiyn

F

Fable noun	داستان	daastaan
Fabric	کپڑا	kaprhaa
Fabulous	شاندار	shaandaar
Face	چہرہ	chehra
Face	سامنا کرنا	saamna karnaa
Face noun	صورت	suurat
Face noun	رخ	rokh
Facilitate	سہل کرنا	sehel karna
Facilitate	امداد کرنا	imdaad karna
Facility	سہولت	sahoolat
Fact	حقیقت	haqiqat
Faction	گروہ	garoh
Factory	کارخانہ	kaarkhaana
Faculty	قابلیت	qaabliyat
Fade	مدھم مڑنا	madham parna
Fail	ہارنا	haarna

Failure	ناکامی	naa-kaami
Faint	بےہوش ہونا	bayhosh hona
Fair	منصفانہ	munsifana
Fair	میلہ	maylaa
Fair	خوب صورت	khoob soorat
Fair	بے عیب	be ayb
Fairy	پری	pari
faisal name; male	فیصل	faisal
Faith	یقین	yaqeen
Fake	نقل	naqal
Falcon	شاہباز	shahbaaz
Fall	گرنا	girna
Fall	آبشار	aabshaar
Fall	ڈھلان	dhalaan
False	غلط	ghalat
Fame	شہرت	shohrat
Familiar	جانا پہچانا	jaana pehchana

Family	فیملی	family
Family	خاندان	khandaan
Famine	قحط	qehet
Famous	مشہور	mashhoor
Fan	پنکھا	pankhaa
fancy like	پسند کرنا	pasnd kerna
fantastic adjective	زبردست	zabardast
Far	دوردراز	dur daraaz
Far	فاصلے پر	faaslay per
Farewell	الوداع	alwidaa
Farm	کھیت	khayt
Farmer	کسان	kisaan
Farming	کھیتی باڑی	khayti-baarhi
fart noun	پھسکی	puskee
Fascinating Adjective	دلکش	Dilkash
Fast	تیز	tayz
Fast	روزہ رکھنا	roza rakhna
Fasten	باندھنا	baandhna

Fasting	روزہ رکھنا	rozaah rakhna
Fat	چربی	charbee
Fat	موٹا	mota
Fatal	مہلک	muhlik
fate noun	قسمت	qismat
Father	والد	waalid
Father	باپ	baap
Father noun; informal	ابو	abbu
fatigue noun	تھکن	fatigue
Fault	خرابی	kharaabi
Favor	عنایت	inaayat
Favor	طرف داری	tarfdaari
Favor	امدادکرنا	imdaad karna
Favor	حمایت کرنا	himaayat karna
Favour	مہربانی	maharbaani
Favourable	مفید	mufeed
Favourite	پسندیدہ	pasandeeda

Fear	خوف	khof
Fear	ڈرنا	darna
Feature	صورت	soorat
February	فروری	february
Feeble	کمزور	kamzor
Feed	پرورش کرنا	parwarish karna
Feed	کھلانا	khilana
Feed	چارہ	chaara
Feed	خوراک	khoraak
Feel	محسوس کرنا	mehsoos karna
Feel	محسوس ہونا	mehsoos hona
Feeling	احساس	ehsaas
Feet	پیر	payr
Fell verb; past tense of fall	گرا	gira
Felony	سنگین جرم	sangeen-juram
Felt	نمدہ	namdah
Felt	چمڑہ	chamrha
Felt	محسوس کیا	mehsoos kiya

Female noun	موئنث	mo'annas
Feminine	مؤنث	mo'annas
Fence	آڑ	aarh
Fertile	زرخیز	zarkhaiz
Fetch	لانا	laanaa
fever noun	بخار	bhukhaar
Few	کچھ	chand
fiance noun	منگیتر	mangetar
Fiction noun; short fiction story	افسانے	afsanay
Fidelity	ایمان داری	imaan-daari
Fidget	بے چین ہونا	baychen hona
Field	میدان	maydaan
Field	کھیت	khayt
Fierce	خوفناک	khofnaak
Fifteen	پندرہ	pandra
Fifty	پچاس	pachaas
Fig	انجیر	anjeer

Fight	لڑنا	larhna
Fight	لڑائی	larhaee
Figure	شکل	shakal
Figure	مجسمہ	mujasma
Figure	تصویر کھینچنا	tasweer khaynchna
Figure	غوروفکر کرنا	ghor-o-fikr karna
Fill	بھرنا	bharna
Film	فلم	film
Filthy	میلا	mela
Final	آخری	aakhri
Final	حتمی	hatmi
Finance	مالیات	maalyaat
Find	ڈھونڈنا	dhoondna
Find	معلوم کرنا	maaloom karna
Fine	جرمانہ	jurmaana
Fine	عمدہ	umda
Fine	نفیس	nafees
Finger	انگلی	oonglee

Finish	ختم کرنا	khatam karna
Finish	مکمل کرنا	mukammal karna
Finite	محدود	mehdood
Fire	آگ	aag
Fire	آگ لگانا	aag lagana
Fire	آگ لگنا	aag lagna
Fire	گولی چلانا	goli chalaana
Fire	غصہ کرنا	ghussa karna
Firm	مضبوط	mazbooth
First	اول	awwal
First	پہلا	pehla
First	پہلے	pehlay
Fish	مچھلی	machhli
Fish	مچھلی پکڑنا	machhli pakarhna
Fishbone noun	مچھلی کا کانٹا	machhli ka kanta
Fisherman noun	ماہیگیر	maaheegeer
Fist	مکا	mukka

Fit	موزوں	mozoon
Fit	قابل	qaabil
Fit	بیماری کا حملہ	beemaaree ka hamla
Fitness	مناسبت	munaasibaat
Five	پانچ	paanch
Fix	ٹھیک کرنا	theek karna
Flabbergast	حیران ہونا	hayraan hona
Flag	جھنڈا	jhanda
Flame	شعلہ	shola
Flammable	بھڑک اٹھنے والا	bharak uthnay wala
Flank	پہلو	pehlu
Flannel	فلالین	flannel
Flap	پھڑپھڑانا	phar-pharaana
Flare	شولے کی چمک	sholay ki chamak
flare verb	بھڑکانا	bharhkana
Flash	چمک	chamak
Flat	ہموار	hamwaar
Flat	چپٹا	chipta

Flatten	ہموار بنانا	hamwaar banaana
flatter verb; impress by speech	چاپلوسی	chaaplosi
Flaw	عیب	eb
Flee	بھاگنا	bhaagna
Flesh	گوشت	gosht
Flight	اڑان	uraan
Fling	پھینکنا	phenkna
Flip	الٹانا	ultaana
flirt verb	دکھاوے کی محبت	dikhave ki mohabbt
Float	تیرنا	tayrnaa
Flock	ریوڑ	raywar
Flood	سیلاب	saylaab
Floor	فرش	farsh
Floor	منزل	manzil
Floored	دبا دینا	dabaa dena
Flourish	پھلنا پھولنا	phalna phoolna
Flow	بہنا	behna

Flow	بہاؤ	bahao
Flower	پھول	phool
fluent adjective	رواں	rawaan
Fluff	نرم رواں	naram ruwaan
Fluorescent	چمکدار	chamakdaar
Flute	بانسری	baansari
Fly	اڑنا	urhna
Fly	اڑانا	urhaana
Fly	مکھی	makhkhee
Foam	جھاگ	jhaag
Focus	دہان	dehaan
Fog	دھند	dhund
Fold	تہ کرنا	teh karna
Foliage	پتے	pattay
Follow	پیچھا کرنا	peechha karna
Follow	تعاقب کرنا	taaqub karna
Follow	پیروی کرنا	payrawi karna

following	مندرجہ ذیل	manderja zeel
adjective Fond	پسند کرنا	pasand karna
Food	خوراک	khoraak
Food noun	کھانا	khaanaa
Fool	بےوقوف	bay-waqoof
Foolish	بے وقوف	bay-waqoof
Foot	پاؤں	paon
Foot	قدم	qadam
Foot	جڑ	jarh
Foot	بنیاد	bunyaad
football noun	فٹ بال	football
For	برائے	baraae
For	کے لئے	kay liyay
For	غرض سے	gharaz say
Forbid	منع کرنا	manaa karna
Force	طاقت	taaqat
Force	زور	zor

Force	جبر	jabar
Force	زبردستی کرنا	zabardasti karna
Force	زور لگانا	zor lagaana
Fore	اگلا	agla
Forehead	پیشانی	payshaani
Foreign	غیر ملکی	ghayr mulki
foreign adjective	بیرونی	bayrooni
Forest	جنگل	jangal
Forever	ہمیشہ کے لئے	hamaysha kay-liay
Forge	نقل کرنا	naqal karna
Forgery	نقل	naqal
Forget	بھولنا	bhulna
Forgive	معاف کرنا	maaf karna
Forgiveness	بخشش	bakhshish
forgot verb; past tense	بھول گیا	bhool gia
Fork	کانٹا	kaanta
Form	فارم	form

Form	ہیئت	hayat
Form	شکل صورت	shakal soorat
Form	بنانا	banana
Form	ترتیب دینا	tarteeb dayna
Formal	رسمی	rasmi
Former	پچھلا	pichla
fortune noun	قسمت	qismat
Forty	چالیس	chaalees
Forward	اگلا	aglaa
Forward	آگے	aagay
Found	بنیاد رکھنا	bunyaad rakhna
Foundation	بنیاد	bunyaad
Fountain	فوارہ	fawaara
Four	چار	char
Fourteen	چودہ	choda
Fourth	چوتھا	chotha
Fowl	پرندہ	parinda
Fox	لومڑی	lomri

Foxy	چالباز	chaalbaaz
Fraction	جز	juz
Fraction	جزوی	juzwee
Fraction	کسر	kasar
Fragile	نازک	naazuk
Fragment	ٹکڑا	tukra
Fragrance	خوشبو	khushboo
Fragrant	خوشبودار	khushbu-daar
Frail	ناذک	naazuk
France	فرانس	france
Frank	صاف گو	saaf go
Fraud	دھوکا	dhoka
Freak noun	غیر معمول	ghayr mamool
Free	آزاد	aazaad
Free	آزاد کرنا	aazaad karna
Free	آزاد ہونا	aazaad hona
Freedom	آزادی	azaadi

Freeze	جمانا	jamaana
French	فرانسیسی	francisi
Frenzy	پاگل پن	pagal-pan
Frequency	کثرت	kasrat
Frequent	اکثر	aksar
Frequently	بکثرت	bakasrat
Fresh	تازہ	taaza
Fresh	تازہ دم	taza dam
Friction	رگڑ	ragar
Friday	جمعہ	juma
Friend	دوست	dost
Friendly	دوستانہ	dostaana
Friendship	دوستی	dosti
Fright	دہشت	dehshat
Frighten	ڈرانا	daraana
Frog	مینڈک	mayndak
Frolic	کھیل کود	khayl kood

From	منجانب	minjaanib
Front	سامنے	saamnay
Front	اگلا	aglaa
Front	سامنا کرنا	saamna karna
Front	میدان جنگ	maydaan-e-jang
Frontier	سرحد	sarhad
Frost	پالا	paala
Frosty	یخ	yakh
Froth	جھاگ	jhaag
Frown	تیوری چڑھانا	tevri charhana
Frozen	منجمد	munjamid
Frugal	کفایت شعاری	kafaayat shay'aari
Fruit	پھل	phal
Fruit	انعام	inaam
Fruit	حاصل	haasil
Frustrate	مایوس ہونا	maayoos hona
Frustration	مایوسی	mayoosi
Fry	تلنا	talna

Fuel	ایندھن	eendhan
Fugitive	مفرور	mafroor
Fulfil	مکمل کرنا	mukammal karna
Fulfilment	تکمیل	takmeel
Full	بھراہوا	bharaa hua
Full	بھرنا	bharnaa
Fumble	ٹٹولنا	tatolna
Fume	دھواں	dhuwaan
Fuming	غصےسےبھرا	ghussay se bhara
Fun	مزاح	mazaah
Fun	تماشا	tamaasha
Fun	تفریح	tafreeh
Fun	مزاق	mazaaq
Function	کام	kaam
Fundamental	بنیادی	bunyaadi
Funeral	جنازہ	janaaza
Funnel	قیف	qeef

Funny	دلچسپ	dilchasp
Furious	غضبناک	ghazabnaak
Furnace	بھٹی	bhatti
Furnish	آراستہ کرنا	aaraasta karna
Further adjective	مزید	mazeed
Fury	غصہ	ghussa
Fuse	پگھلنا	pighlaana
Fuss	ہنگامہ	hangaama
Futile	بیکار	baykaar
Futility	بے کارکردگی	bay-kaarkardagi
Future	مستقبل	mustaqbil

G

gabby Noun; name	گیبی	Gabby
Gadget	چھوٹا آلہ	chota aala
Gain	نفع	nafa
Galaxy	کہکشاں	kehkeshan
Gale	آندھی	aandhi
Gamble	جوا	jua
Game	کھیل	khayl
Game	شکار	shikaar
Games	کھیل	khayl
Gang	گروہ	giroh
Garbage	کوڑاکرکٹ	kura karkat
Garden	باغ	baagh
Gargle	غرارے	gharaaray
Garlic	لہسن	lassan
Gas	گیس	gas
Gash	گہرا زخم	gehra zakham

Gasoline	پٹرول	petrol
Gasp	ہانپنا	haanpna
Gate	دروازہ	darwaaza
Gather	جمع کرنا	jamaa karna
Gather	اکھٹے کرنا	ikatthay karna
Gather	جمع ہونا	jamaa hona
Gave	دیا	diya
Gave	عطاکیا	ataa kiya
Gay	خوش	khush
Gaze	گھورنا	ghoorna
gender male or female	جنس	jender
General	جرنیل	general
General	عام	aam
General	عمومی	amomi
Generous	سخی	sakhi
Genocide	نسل کشی	nasal-kashi
Gentle	نرم مزاج	narm mizaaj

Gentle	حلیم	haleem
Gentle	شریف	shareef
Gentleman	شریف آدمی	shareef aadmi
Genuine	اصلی	asli
Geography	جغرافیہ	geography
Germ	جرثومہ	jarsuma
Get	حاصل کرنا	haasil karna
getting verb; the act of acquiring	حاصل کرنا	hasil karna
Ghost	بھوت	bhoot
Giant	دیو	dio
Giddy	چکراتا	chakraataa
Gift	تحفہ	tohfa
Gigantic	بہت بڑا	bahot bara
Giggle	دبی ہوی ہنسی	dabi hui hansi
Ginger	ادرک	adrak
Giraffe	زرافہ	ziraafa
Girl	لڑکی	larhki

Gist	خلاصہ	khulaasa
Give	دینا	dayna
Given	دیا گیا	diaa giaa
Glad	خوش	khush
Glamour	نظرفریب	nazar-farayb
Glance	جھلک	jhalak
Glare	تیز روشنی	tayz roshni
Glass	گلاس	glass
Glass	شیشہ	shisha
Glass	کانچ	kaanch
Glasses	عینک	aynak
Gleam	چمک	chamak
Glide	پھسلنا	phisalna
Glimmer	چمکتی روشنی	chamakti roshni
Glimpse	جھلک	jhalak
Glint	چمک	chamak
Glitter	چمک	chamak

Global	دنیا بھر کی	dunya bhar ki
Gloomy	اداس	udaas
Glorious	شاندار	shaandaar
Glory	عظمت	azmat
Glove	دستانہ	dastaana
Glow	دمکنا	damakna
Glue	گوند	gond
Glum	ناخوشی	naa-khush
Go	جانا	jaana
Go	جاؤ	jao
Goal	منزل	manzil
Goat	بکری	bakri
Goblin	بونا	bona
God	خدا	khuda
Going	جا رہے	ja rahaay
Gold	سونا	sona
Gold	زر	zar
Golden	سنہری	sunehri

Golden adjective	زرین	zareen
Gone	چلاگیا	chala gaya
Gone	گزرا ہوا	guzra hua
gonna verb	ہونا	hona
Good	اچھا	achhchha
Good	عمدہ	umda
Goodbye	الوداع	alwidaah
goodbye interjection; God Bless	خدا حافظ	Khuda Hafiz
Goodnight	شب بخیر	shab-bakhayr
Goods	اشیاء	ashyaa
google noun	گوگل	google
Gorgeous	دلکش	dilkash
Gossip	افواہ	afwaah
Got	حاصل کیا	haasil kiya
Govern	حکومت کرنا	hukumat karna
Govern	نگرانی کرنا	nigraani karna
Government	حکومت	hakoomat

Grab	جکڑنا	jakarna
Graceful	حسین	haseen
Gradual	دھیرے	dheeray
Gradually	دھیرے دھیرے	dheeray dheeray
Grain	ذرہ	zarra
Grand	اعلی	aala
Grand	عظیم	azeem
Grandchild	پوتا	pota
Grandfather	دادا	daadaa
Grandmother	دادی	daadi
Grant	بخشنا	bakhshna
Grape	انگور	angoor
Grasp	مضبوطی سے پکڑنا	mazbooti say pakarna
Grass	گھاس	ghaas
Grasshopper	ٹڈا	tidda
Grateful	شکرگزار	shukar guzaar
Gratitude	شکرانہ	shukraana

Grave	قبر	qabar
Gravel	بجری	bajri
Gravity	کشش	kashish
Gravy	شوربہ	shorba
Gray	سرمئی	surmai
Graze	رگڑ لگنا	ragar lagna
grazer noun	چراک	charaak
Grease	چکنائی	chiknaai
Great	شاندار	shaandar
Great	عظیم	azeem
Greece	یونان	yu-naan
Greed	لالچ	laalach
Greedy	لالچی	laalchi
Greek	یونانی	yu-naani
Green	سبز	sabz
Green	ہرا	haraa
Green	سرسبز	sar sabz

Greet	استقبال	istaqbaal
Greeting	مبارکبادی	mubaarak-baadi
Greetings	مبارکباد	mubaarak-baad
Grew	بڑا ہوا	barha hua
Grew	پروان چڑھا	parwaan charha
Grief	غم	gham
Grievance Noun	شکوی	Shikwa
Grill	سیخدار چولھا	seekhdaar chula
Grin	مسکراہٹ	muskuraahat
Grind	پیسنا	peesna
Grip	گرفت	grift
Groan	کراہنا	karaahna
Grope	ٹٹولنا	tatolna
Ground	میدان	maydaan
Ground	زمین	zamin
Grounded	پسا ہوا	pisaa hua
groundless adjective	بے بنیاد	bebunyaad

Group	گروه	groh
Group	جماعت	jamaat
Group	ترتیب دینا	tarteeb dena
Group	جماعت بندی کرنا	jamaatbandi karna
Grow	اگنا	ugna
Grow	اگانا	ugaana
Grow	پروان چڑھنا	parwaan charhna
Grow	ترقی کرنا	taraqqi karna
Growl	غرانا	ghurraana
Grudge	دشمنی	dushmani
Guard	دربان	darbaan
Guardian	سرپرست	sarparast
Guava Noun	امرود	Umrooth
Guess	اندازه	andaaza
Guess	اندازه کرنا	andaaza karna
Guest	مہمان	mehmaan
Guidance noun	ہدائت	Hidaayat
Guide	رہنما	rehnuma

Guilt	احساس جرم	ehsaas-e-jurm
Guilty	مجرم	mujrim
Guitar	ستار	sitaar
Gulf	خلیج	khaleej
Gulp	نگلنا	nigalna
Gum	مسوڑھے	masooray
Gun	گن	gun
Gun	بندوق	bandooq
Gust	جھونکا	jhonka
Gutter	نالی	naali
Guy	مرد	mard
Gym noun	جمخانہ	gymkhana
Gym noun	جمخانہ	gymkhana

H

Habit	عادت	aadat
Habitation	مسکن	muskin
Habitual	معمول	ma'mool
Hack	توڑ ڈالنا	torh daalna
Hacker	توڑنے والا	torhnay waala
Had	تھا	tha
Haggard	تھکا ہوا	thaka hua
Haha	ہا ہا	haha
Hail	اولے	olay
Hailstone	اولا	ola
Hair	بال	baal
Half	آدھا	aadha
Half	نصف	nisf
Hall	بڑا کمرہ	barha kamra
Halt	ٹھہرنا	therna
Halve	آدھاکرنا	aadha karna

Hammer	ہتھوڑا	hathorha
hamza noun; name	حمزہ	hamza
Hand	ہاتھ	haath
Hand	حوالے کرنا	hawalay karna
Handcuff	ہتھکڑی	hathkarhi
Handicap	رعایت	ray'aayat
Handicraft	کاریگری	kaarigari
Handkerchief	رومال	romaal
Handle	استعمال کرنا	istamal karna
handover noun	حوالگی	havaalgi
Handsome	خوبصورت	khubsoorat
Hang	لٹکانا	latkaana
Happen	واقع ہونا	waqay hona
Happiness	خوشی	khushi
Happy	خوش	khush
Harbour	بندرگاہ	bandargaah
Hard	سخت	sakht

Hardliner	سخت	sakht
Hardly	بمشکل	baa-mushkil
Hardly	مشکل سے	mushkil say
Hare	خرگوش	khargosh
Harm	نقصان	nuqsaan
harmony noun	ہم آہنگی	hum aahang
Harsh	درشت	durusht
Harvest	فصل کاٹنا	fasal kaatna
Has	ہے	hay
Haste	جلدی کرنا	jaldi karna
Hat	ٹوپی	topee
Hate	نفرت کرنا	nafrat karna
Hatred	نفرت	nafrat
Haughty	مغرور	mughroor
Haul	کھینچنا	khaynchna
Have	رکھنا	rakhnaa
Hawk	عقاب	uqaab

Hazard	خطرہ	khatraa
Hazardous	خطرناک	khatarnaak
Haze	گردو غبار	gard-o-ghubar
He	وہ	woh
Head	سر	sar
Head	سربراہ	sarbaraah
Headache	سردرد	sar dard
Heal	زخم بھرنا	zakham bharna
Health	صحت	sayhat
Healthy	صحتمند	sayhat mand
Heap	ڈھیر	dhayr
Hear	سننا	sunna
Heard	سنا	suna
Heart	دل	dil
Heart noun	قلب	Qalb
Hearth	چولھا	choolha
Heartless	بےدل	bay-dil

Heat	گرمی	garmi
Heat	گرم کرنا	garm karna
Heaven	جنت	jannat
Heavenly noun	آسمانی	aasmaani
Heavy	بھاری	bhaari
Heavy	وزنی	wazni
hectic adjective	بہت مصروف	bohat masroof
Heel	ایڑی	ayrhee
Height	اونچائی	unchaai
Heir	وارث	waaris
Held	پکڑا	pakrhaa
Held	تھاما	thaama
Hell	دوزخ	dozakh
Hell noun	جہنم	Jahannum
Hello	آداب	adaab
Hello	سلام	salaam
Help	مدد	madad

Help	مدد کرنا	madad karnaa
Helpless	مجبور	majboor
Hence	اس سبب	is sabab
Henna noun	مہندی	Mehendi
Henna noun	حنا	Hina
Her	اس کا	oos kaa
Herd	ڑیوڑ	raywar
Here	یہاں	yahaan
Heritage	ورثہ	virsa
Hesitate	ہچکچانا	hichkichaana
Hesitation	ہچکچاہٹ	hichkichaahat
Hey	ارے	hey
Hi	آداب	adaab
Hi	سلام	salaam
Hiccup	ہچکی	hichki
hidden adjective	چھپا	chuppa

hidden	پوشیدہ	posheedah
adjective		
Hide	چھپانا	chupana
High	اونچا	oonchaa
High	بلند	baland
Highwayman	راہزن	raahzan
Hijack	اغوا	aghwa
Hill	پہاڑ	pahaarh
Him	اس کو	oos ko
Hind	پچھلا	pichla
Hinder	رکاوٹ	rokaawat
Hindu	ہندو	hindu
Hinduism	ہندومت	hindu-mat
Hint	اشارہ	ishaara
Hip noun	کولھا	koolha
Hire	کرائے پر لینا	karaay par layna
His	اس کا	oos ka

History	تاریخ	taareekh
Hit	مارنا	maarna
Hit	ضرب لگانا	zarb lagana
Hit	ضرب	zarb
Hobby	شوک	shok
hockey noun; game	هالي	haly
Hold	پکڑنا	pakarhnaa
Hold	تھامنا	thaamna
Hold	قائم رہنا	qaaim rayhna
Hole	سوراخ	suraakh
Hole	گڑھا	garhhaa
Hole	سوراخ کرنا	sooraakh karna
Holiday	چھٹی	chhutti
Hollow	کھوکھلا	khokla
Holy	مقدس	muqaddas
Home	گھر	ghar
Homicide	قتل	qatal

homosexual noun	حم جنس پسند	hum jins pasand
Honest	ایماندار	imaandaar
Honesty	سچائی	sacchaai
Honey	شہد	shehed
Honour	اعزاز	ayzaaz
Hoof	کھر	khur
Hook	کانٹا	kaanta
Hope	امید	ummeed
Hope	امید کرنا	ummeed karna
Hope	توقع رکھنا	tawaqqo rakhnaa
Hopeless	مایوس کن	mayooskun
Horizon	افق	afaq
Horizontal	افقی	ufaqqi
Horn	سینگ	seeng
Horn	ہارن	horn
Horny	سینگ جیسا	seeng jesa
Horrible	وحشتناک	wehshat-naak

Horror	وحشت	wehshat
Horse	گھوڑا	ghoraa
Horseshoe	نعل	naal
Hospital	ہسپتال	hospital
hospitality noun	مہمان نوازی	mehaman nawazi
Host	میزبان	mayzbaan
Hostage	یرغمالی	yarghamaali
Hostile adjective	مخالف	mukhalaf
Hot	گرم	garm
Hot	پرجوش	purjosh
Hour	گھنٹا	ghantaa
Hour	وقت	waqt
House	مکان	makaan
House	رہائش گاہ	rahaaish gah
How	کیسے	kaysay
however adverb	لیکن	laykin
however conjunction	مگر	magar

Howl	چیخنا	cheekhna
hubby noun	شوہر	shohar
Huddle	ٹھنس جانا	thuns jaana
Hug	گلے لگانا	galay lagaana
Huge	بہت بڑا	bohot barhaa
Huge	وسیع	wasee
Hull	دھانچہ	dhaancha
Hum	گنگنانا	gungunaana
Human	آدمی	aadmee
Human	انسان	insaan
Human	انسانی	insaani
Humane	نرم دل	naram dil
Humanity	انسانیت	insaaniyat
Humble	آجزی	aajazi
Humbug	فریب	farayb
Humidity	نمی	nami
Humiliate	ذلیل کرنا	zaleel karna

Humiliation	ذلت	zillat
Humility	عاجزی	aajazi
Humour	مزاق	mazaaq
Hump	کوہان	kohaan
Hunch	ٹیڑ	terh
Hundred	سو	so
Hunger	بھوک	bhook
Hungry	بھوکا	bhooka
Hunt	شکار کرنا	shikaar karna
Hunt	ڈھونڈنا	dhoondna
Hurl	دور پھینکنا	dur phaynkna
Hurricane noun	طوفان	tufaan
Hurry	جلدی کرنا	jaldi karna
Hurry	جلدی	jaldee
Hurt	درد کرنا	dard karna
Husband	شوہر	shohar
Hush	چپ کرنا	chup karna
Hustle	دھکم بازی	dhakkam baazi

Hypocrisy	فريب	farayb
hypocrite noun	منافق	munafiq

I

I	میں	mayn
Ice	برف	barf
Idea	خیال	kheyaal
Ideal	تصوری	tasawwuri
Identical	یکساں	yaksaan
Identity	پہچان	pehchaan
Idiot	بے وقوف	bay waqoof
Idle	سست	sust
Idol	بت	but
If	اگر	agar
If	کاش	kaash
Ignite	جلانا	jalaana
Ignorant	جاہل	jaahil
Ignore	نظر انداز کرنا	nazar andaaz karna
Ill	بیمار	bimaar
illegal forbidden by law or statute	غیر قانونی	Gayr qanooni
illiterate noun; unable to read and write	جاہل	jahil

Illness	بیماری	bimaari
Illumination	روشن کرنا	roshan karna
illusion noun	فریب نظر	fareb-i-nazar
Illustration	تصویر	tasweer
Imaginary	خیالی	khiyaali
Imagination	خیال	khiyaal
Imagine	سوچنا	sochna
Imagine	تصور کرنا	tasawwur karna
Imagine	خیال کرنا	khayaal karna
Imitate	نقل کرنا	naqal karna
Immaculate	بے عیب	bay-eb
Immature	ناپختہ	naa-pukhta
Immediate	فوری	fori
Immediately	فوراً	foran
Immense	بہت زیادہ	bohot ziyaada
Imminent	آمد ہونے والا	aamad honay wala
Immortal	لازوال	la-zawal
impact verb	اثر	asar
Impatient	بےصبر	bay sabr

Implement	نافذ کرنا	naafiz karna
Implore	درخواست	darkhuaast
importance noun	اہمیت	ahmiyat
Important	اہم	ehem
Impossible	ناممکن	naa-mumkin
Impress	متاثر	mutaasir
Impression	اثر	asar
Impressive	پر اثر	pur-asar
Imprison	قیدکرنا	qayd karna
Improve	بہترکرنا	behtar karna
Imran noun; name	عمران	Imran
In	اندر	andar
In	شامل ہونا	shaamil hona
Inaugration	افتتاح	iftaytaah
Incense	خوشبودار	khushbudaar
Inch	انچ	inch
Include	شامل کرنا	shaamil karna
Include	شامل ہونا	shaamil hona
include verb	مشتمل ہونا	musthamil hona

income	آمدنی	aamdani
noun incomparable adj	بمسال	bay-misaal
Incontinence noun	مشانے کی کمذور	maana ki kamzori
Inconvenience	دقت	dikkat
Incorporate	اکھٹا کرنا	akhatta karna
Incorrect	غلط	galat
Increase	بڑھانا	barhaana
Incredible	ناقابل یقین	naa-qabil-e-yaqeen
Indeed	یقیناً	yaqeenan
Independence	آزادی	aazaadi
Independent	آزاد	aazaad
India	بھارت	bhaarat
Indicate	ظاہر کرنا	zahir karna
Indicate	نشاندہی کرنا	nishaandahi karna
Indicate	اشارہ کرنا	ishara karna
Indicator noun	اشارہ	ishaaraa
Indicator noun; car's indicator	برقی قمقمی برائے تبدیلئ رخ	Barqi qumqumi barah-e-tabdeel-e-rukh
Indignant	خفا	khafaa

Indispensable	ناگزیر	naa-guzeer
Individual	شخصی	shakhsi
Indoor	اندر	andar
indulge verb	لطف اٹھانا	lutf uthana
Industry	صنعت	sanat
Infant	کمسن بچہ	kamsin bachcha
Infectious	متعدی	mutaa'di
Infinite	لامحدود	laa-mehdood
inflation price increases	قیمتیں بڑھنا	price increases
influence verb	اثر کرنا	asar karna
Info	معلومات	maa'lumaat
Inform	اطلاع	itlaa dayna
Informal	غیر رسمی	ghayr-rasmi
Information	معلومات	maa'lumaat
Infrastructure	اساس	asaas
Infuriate	غصہ دلانا	ghussa dilaana
Initial	ابتدائی	ibtaydaai
Injure	زخمی	zakhmi
Injury	زخم	zakham
Ink	روشنائی	roshnaai

Inn	سرائے	suraa-ay
Innocent	معصوم	maasoom
Innovation	ایجاد	ijaad
Innumerable adjective	بیشمار	bishomaar
Inquiry	تفتیش	tafteesh
insane adjective	پاگل	pagal
insane adjective	غیر دانشمند	ghair danishmand
Insect	کیڑا	keerha
Inside	اندر	andar
Insist	اصرار	israar
Insolent	گستاخ	gustaakh
Inspect	ملاحظہ کرنا	mulaahiza karna
inspiration noun	تخلیقی کام کی تحریک	takhleeqi kam ki tahreek
inspire verb	دل میں ڈالنا	dil mein daalna
Install	نصب کرنا	nasab karna
Installation	تنصیب	tanseeb
Instalment	قسط	qist
instance noun	مسال کے طورپہ	mesaal k toor peh
Instant	فوری	fori

Instant	لمحہ	lamha
Instant	وقت	waqt
Instantly	فوراً	foran
Instead	بجائے	bajaay
Instruct	ہدایت دینا	hidaayat dayna
Instruction	ہدایت	hadaayat
Instrument	آلہ	aala
Instrument	اوزار	ozaar
Instrument	ساز	saaz
Insult	بے عزت کرنا	bay izzat karna
Integral	کامل	kaamil
Integrate	جمع کرنا	jamaa karna
Integrity	دیانت	diyaanat
Intellect	سمج	samajh
Intellectual	اقلی	aqli
Intelligence	خبر	khabar
Intelligent	ذہین	zaheen
Intelligible	قابل فہم	qabil-e-fehem
Intend	نیت رکھنا	niyyat rakhna

Intense	شدید	shadeed
Intensity	شدت	shiddat
Intent	مشغول	mashghool
Intention	ارادہ	iraada
Interact	گفتگو کرنا	guftagu karna
Interactive	آمنے سامنے	aamnay-saamnay
Intercourse verb	مباشرت	mubasharat
Interest	اثر	asar
Interest	دلچسپی	dilchaspi
Interest	نفع	nafa
Interest	دلچسپی ہونا	dilchaspi hona
interest noun	مفاد	mafaad
interesting adjective; a sense of attraction for something	دلچسپ	dilchasp
interface noun	انٹرفیس	interface
Interfere	مداخلت	mudaakhilat
Interim	درمیانا عرصہ	darmiyaana arsa
internal adjective	اندرونی	andhrooni
International	بین الاقوامی	bayn ul aqwaami
Internet	انٹرنیٹ	internet
Interpret	تفصیر کرنا	tafseer karna

Interpret	تفسیر	tafseer
Interrupt	مداخلت کرنا	mudaakhilat karna
Interval	وقفہ	waqfa
Intervention	مداخلت	mudaakhilat
Interview	انٹرویو	interview
Into	میں	mein
Introduce	ملاقات کرانا	mulaaqaat karaana
Invade	چڑھائی کرنا	charhaai karna
Invalid	معزور	maa'zoor
Invent	ایجاد کرنا	eejad karna
Invent	تخلیق کرنا	takhliq karna
Invention	ایجاد	ijaad
inventory verb	فہرست تیارکرنا	fahrist tayaar karna
Invert	الٹا کرنا	ultaa karna
Inverted	الٹا	ulta
Investigate	تفتیش کرنا	tafteesh karna
Investigation	تفتیش	tafteesh
Invisible	پوشیدہ	posheeda
Invitation	دعوت نامہ	daawat naama

Invite	دعوت	daa'wat
Invoke	بلانا	bulaana
Involve verb	شامل کرنا	shaamil karna
involved verb	ملوس ہونا	mullawis hona
irfan noun; male name	عرفان	irfan
Iron	لوہا	loha
Iron	استری	istiri
Iron	استری کرنا	istiri karna
Iron noun	آہن	aahan
Ironsmith	لوہار	lohaar
Ironsmith noun	آہنگر	aahan-gar
Irony	طنز	tanz
Irrational	خلاف عقل	khilaaf-e-aqal
Irrecognizable	ناقابل شناخت	na-qaabil-e-shanaakht
Irreducible	ناقبل تخفیف	na-qaabil-e-takhfeef
Irregular	بے قاعدہ	bay-qaaida
irregularity noun	بے ضابطگی	bezabtagi
Irrelative	بےربط	bay-rabt
Irrelevant	غیرمتعلق	ghayr-mutalliq
Irritate	تنگ کرنا	tang karna

Is	ہے	hay
Islam	اسلام	islam
Island	جزیرہ	jazeera
issue verb	اجراء کرنا	ijra karna
It	یہ	yay
Italy	اطالیہ	italy
Itch	کھجلی	khujli
Item	شے	shay
Its	اس کا	us kaa
Itself	بذات خود	ba'zaat-e-khud

J – K

Jabber	بکبک کرنا	bak bak karna
Jack	جیک	jack
Jackal	گیدڑ	geedar
Jackass	گدھا	gadha
Jackdaw	کوا	kawa
Jacket	جاکٹ	jacket
Jag	دانتا	daanta
Jagged	دندانددار	dandaandaar
Jail	جیل	jail
Jailer	جیلر	jailer
Jam	جکڑنا	jakarna
Jangle	جھنجھنانا	jhunjhunaana
January	جنوری	january
Japan	جپان	japan
Jar	صراحی	suraahi

Jargon	بولی جو سمجھ نہ آئے	boli jo samajh na aa'ay
Jasmine	یاسمین	jasmine
Jaunt	گھومنا	ghumna
Jaw	جبڑا	jabara
Jay	نیل کنٹھ	neel kunt
Jealous	حاسد	haasid
Jealously	حسد	hasad
Jeer	طعنہ مارنا	taa'na maarna
Jelly	جیلی	jelly
Jeopardise	خطرے میں ڈالنا	khatray mein daalna
Jeopardy	اندیشہ	andesha
Jerk	جھٹکا	jhatka
Jersey	اونی کرتا	ooni kurta
Jess	بندھن	bandhan
Jest	مزاق	mazaaq
Jesus	عیسی	eesa
Jet	تیز دھار	tez dhaar

Jew	یہودی	yahoodi
Jewel	زیور	zaywar
Jewellery	زیور	zaywar
Jilt	دھوکے باز	dhokay baaz
Jingle	جھنجھنانا	jhunjhunaana
Job	جاب	job
Job	نوکری	nokree
Jock	جوک	jock
Jockey	جوکی	jockey
Jog	جوگ	jog
Join	جوڑنا	jorhna
Join	ملانا	milana
Join	شامل کرنا	shamil karna
Join	شامل ہونا	shamil hona
Joint	جوڑ	jorh
joint adjective	مشترکہ	mushtarka
Joke	لطیفہ	lateefa

Joker	مزاق کرنے والا	mazaak karnay wala
Jolt	جھٹکا	jhatka
Jostle	دھکا دینا	dhakka dena
Jot	ذرہ	zarra
Journal	رسالہ	rasaala
Journalism	صحافت	sahaafat
Journalist	صحافی	sahaafi
Journey	سفر	safar
Jovial	خوش مزاج	khush-mizaaj
Joy	خوشی	khushi
Jubilation	خوشی	khushi
Judaism	یہودیت	yahoodiyyat
Judge	قاضی	qaazi
Judgement	فیصلہ	faysala
Judicial	عدالتی	adaalati
Judiciary	منصف	munsif
Jug	صراحی	saraahi

Jugular	گردن کا	gardan ka
Juice	رس	ras
Juicy	رسیلا	raseela
July	جلائی	july
Jumble	بےترتیب	bay-tarteeb
Jump	چھلانگ	chhalaang
Jump	چھلانگ لگانا	chhalaag lagaana
Jump	کودنا	koodna
Junaid noun; name	جنید	junaid
Junction	جوڑ	jorh
June	جون	june
Jungle	جنگل	jungle
Junior	چھوٹا	chota
Junk	کباڑ	kabaarh
Jupiter	مشتری	mishtari
Juridical	قانونی	qaanuni
Jurisdiction	اختیار	ikhtiyaar

Just	منصف	munsif
Just	منصفانہ	munsifaana
Just	محض	mehez
Just	ابھی ابھی	abhi abhi
Justice	انصاف	insaaf
Justify	جواز دینا	jawaaz dena
kashif noun; name	کاشف	kashif
Keen	شوقین	shoqeen
Keep	رکھنا	rakhna
Keep	سنبھالنا	sanbhaalna
Kept	رکھا	rakhkha
Kept	سنبھالا	sanbhala
Kernel	مرکز	markaz
Key	چابی	chaabi
khan noun; name	خان	khan
Kick	ٹھوکر	thokhar
Kid	بچہ	bacha
Kidnap	اغوا	aghwa

Kidney	گردہ	gurda
Kill	مارنا	maarna
Kill	قتل کرنا	qatl karna
Kiln	بھٹی	bhatti
Kin	رشتدار	rishtaydaar
Kind	قسم	qism
Kind	مہربان	mehrban
Kindle	جلنا	jalna
Kindred	رشتداری	rishtaydaari
Kinetic	حرکت کی	harkat ki
King	بادشاہ	badshah
Kingdom	ملک	mulk
Kingdom	مملکت	mamlokat
Kinship	رشتداری	rishtaydaari
Kiosk	کھوکھا	khokha
Kiss	پیار	piyaar
Kiss verb	چومنا	choomna

Kitchen	باورچی خانہ	baawarchi khana
Kite	پتنگ	patang
Kitten	بلی کا بچہ	billi ka bacha
Knack	سلیقہ	saleeqa
Knee	گھٹنا	ghutna
Kneel	جھکنا	jhukna
Knew	جانتا تھا	jaanta tha
Knew	پہچانتا تھا	pehchaanta tha
Knife	چھری	churi
Knight	نائٹ	knight
Knight	بہادر	bahaadur
Knit	بننا	bunna
Knock	دستک دینا	dastak dayna
Knot	گرہ	giraah
Know	جاننا	jaanna
Know	پہچاننا	pehchaanna
Know	آگاہ ہونا	aagaah hona

Knowledge	علم	ilm
Known	جانا ہوا	jaana hona
Kurdistan noun; the land of kurds	کردستان	Kurdistan

L

Labour noun	مزدوری	mazduri
Lack	کمی	kami
Ladder	سیڑھی	seerhi
Ladle	چمچہ	chamcha
Lady	لیڈی	lady
Lady	خاتون	khatoon
lahore city of pakistan	لاہور	lahore
Lake	جھیل	jheel
Lamb	میمنا	memna
Lame	لنگڑا	langra
Lamp	چراغ	charaagh
Lance	نیزہ	nayza
Land	زمین	zameen
Land	میدان	maydaan
Land	زمین پر اترنا	zamin per ootarna
Landlord	جاگیردار	jaagirdaar

Landscape	قدرتی مناظر	qudrati manaazir
Landscape	بھاگ جانا	bhaag jaanaa
Landscrap	قدرتی مناظر	qudrati manaazir
Lane	گلی	gali
Language	زبان	zabaan
Language	بولی	bolee
Large	بڑا	barhaa
Last	آخری	aakhree
Last	پچھلا	pichhlaa
Late	تاخیر	taakhir
Late	مرحوم	marhoom
Later	بعد میں	baad mein
Lather	جھاگ	jhaag
Latin	لاطینی	latini
Laugh	ہنسی	hansi
Laugh	ہنسنا	hansnaa
Laughter	ہنسی	hansi

Launch	آغاز	aghaaz
Laundry	دھلائی کے کپڑے	dhulaai kay kapray
Law	قانون	qaanoon
Lawn	باغ	baagh
Lay	رکھنا	rakhnaa
Lay	لٹانا	litana
Lay	بچھانا	bichhaana
Layer	تہہ	teh
Lazy	سست	sust
Lazy adjective	کاہل	kaahil
Lead	سیسہ	seesa
Lead	رہنمائ کرنا	rehnumai karna
Lead	پیشوائی کرنا	peshwai karna
Lead	سرفہرست	sare fehrist
Leader	رہنما	rehnuma
Leaf	پتہ	patta
Leak	شگاف	shigaaf
Lean	جھکنا	jhukna

Leap	چھلانگ	chalaang
Learn	سیکھنا	seekhna
Learned	عالم	aalim
Leash	باندھنے کی ڈوری	baandhnay ki dori
Least	سب سے کم	sab se kam
Least	بہت کم	bohot kam
Leather	چمڑا	chamra
Leave	چھوڑنا	chhorhna
Leave	ترک کرنا	tark karna
Leave	چھٹی	chhutti
Leave	رخصت	rukhsat
Left	بایاں	baayaan
Left	چھوڑا	chhorha
Leg	پاؤں	paaon
Leg	ٹانگ	taang
legacy noun	وراست	waraasat
Legal noun	جائز	Jaaiz

Legend	داستان	daastaan
Legible	پڑنے کے قابل	parnay kay qaabil
legislation noun	قانون	kanoon
Leisure	تفریح	tafreeh
Lemon	لیموں	leemun
Lend	ادھار دینا	udhaar dayna
Length	لمبائی	lambaai
Lengthen	لمبا کرنا	lamba karna
Lens	عدسہ	adsaah
lentil noun	دال	daal
Lesbian noun	ہم جنس پرست	humjins pasand
Lesbian noun	لسبیان	lesbian
Less	کم	kam
Less	بغیر	baghayr
Lessen	کم کرنا	kam karna
Lesson	سبق	sabaq
Let	اجازت دینا	ijaazat dena

Letter	خط	khat
Letter	حرف	harf
lettuce noun; vegetable	سلاد	salaad
Level	سطح	sataah
Level	ہموار	hamwaar
Level	منہدم کرنا	munhadim karna
liability Adjective	ذمہ داری	zimmedaaree
Liar	جھوٹا	jhoota
library noun	کتاب خانہ	kitaab khana
Lick	چاٹنا	chaatna
Lie	جھوٹ	jhoot
Lie	جھوٹ بولنا	jhoot bolna
Lie	لیٹنا	laytna
Life	زندگی	zindagi
Lift	اٹھانا	uthana
Lift	اونچا کرنا	ooncha karna
Light	ہلکا	halka

Light	روشنی	roshni
Light	ہلکا کرنا	halka karna
Light	روشن کرنا	roshan karna
Light	جلانا	jalaana
Light noun	نور	noor
Lighten	وزن کی کمی	wazan ki kami
Lighten	جلانا	jalaana
Lighthouse	روشنی کا مینار	roshnee ka minaar
Lightning	آسمانی بجلی	aasmaani bijli
Like	پسند کرنا	pasand karna
Like	مانند	maanind
Limit	حد	had
Limp	بے جان	bay jaan
Line	لکیر	lakeer
Line	ڈور	dor
Line	رسی	rassi
Line	قطار	qataar
Line	لکیر کھینچنا	lakir khaynchna

Liner	بڑا جہاز	bara jahaaz
Linger	ٹھہرنا	therna
Lining	اندرونی تہہ	andruni teh
Link	جوڑ	jorh
Lion	ببر شیر	babar sher
Lip	ہونٹ	hont
Liquid	مایع	maya
List	فہرست	fehrist
Listen	سننا	sunna
Little	چھوٹا	chhota
Little	تھوڑا	thorha
Live	زندہ	zinda
Live	زندہ رہنا	zinda rehna
Live	زندگی بسر کرنا	zindagi basar karna
Live verb; broadcast	براہ راست	Baraah-e-raast
Lively	خوش دل	khush dil
Liver	جگر	jigar

living noun	جاندار	jandaar
Lizard	چھپکلی	chipkali
Load	سامان	samaan
Loan	قرض	qarz
Local	مقامی	maqaami
Locality	مقام	maqaam
Locate	مقرر کرنا	muqarrar karna
Locate	قائم کرنا	qaaim karna
Locate	نشاندہی کرنا	nishaandahi karna
Location	جگہ	jagah
Lock	تالا	taala
Locket	لاکٹ	locket
Locust	ٹڈی	tiddi
Lodge	مسکن	maskin
Lodging	ٹھہرنا	tehrna
Log	شہتیر	shehteer
Log	درج کرنا	darj karna

Logical Adjective	منطقی	mantiqi
Logical Adjective	قابل تسلیم	qaabil e taslim
Lol	زور کی ہنسی	zor ki hansee
London noun; city	لندن	London
Lone	اکیلا	akayla
Lone	تنہا	tanhaa
Lone	ویران	veeraan
Loneliness	تنہائی	tanhaai
Lonely	تنہا	tanha
Lonesome	تنہا	tanha
Long	لمبا	lambaa
Long	طویل	taweel
Long	خواہش کرنا	khaahish karna
Look	دیکھنا	daykhna
Looking verb	دیکھ رہا	dekh raha
Lookup	ڈھونڈنا	dhundna
Loop	پھندا	phanda

Loophole	سراخ	suraakh
Loose	ڈھیلا	dheela
Loot	مال غنیمت	maal-e-ghaneemat
Lopsided	ناہموار	na-hamwaar
Lord	سردار	sardaar
Lore	فن	fun
Lose	کھونا	khona
Lost	گم شدہ	gumshuda
lot noun	بہت	bohot
lotus widely cultivated for its large pink or white flowers	کنول	lotas
Loud	پرشور	pur shor
Love	محبت	muhabbat
Love	محبت کرنا	muhabbat karna
love noun	عشق	ishq
Lovely	خوبصورت	khubsurat
Lover	چاہنے والا	chahnay waala

Lover	چاہنے والی	chahnay waali
lover noun	ماہی	maahi
loving adjective	لاڈلا	Yeh mera ladla bata hay
Low	نیچا	nicha
Low	کم	kam
Loyal	وفادار	wafaadaar
Luck	قسمت	qismat
Lucky	خوش قسمت	khush qismat
Luggage	سامان	samaan
Lullaby	لوری	lori
Lumberjack	لکڑہارا	lakkar-haara
Lump	سوجن	soojan
Lunch	کھانا	khana
Lung	پھیپھڑا	phaypara
Lust	مستی	masti

M

Machine	مشین	machine
Mad	پاگل	paagal
Madam	بیگم صاحبہ	begum saahiba
Made	بنایا	banaa ya
Made	تیارشدہ	tayyaar-shuda
Madness	پاگل پن	paagal-pan
Magazine	میگزین	magazine
Magazine	رسالہ	risaalaa
Magic	جادو	jaadoo
Magician	جادوگر	jaadu gar
Magistrate	مجسٹریٹ	magistrate
Magnet	مقناطیس	maqnaatis
Magnificence	شان و شوکت	shaan-o-shokat
Magnificent	عالی شان	aali shaan
Magnify	بڑا کرنا	bara karna
Maid	نوکرانی	nokraani

Mail	ڈاک	daak
Main	مرکزی	markazi
Maintain	قائم رکھنا	qaaim rakhna
Maintenance	محافظت	muhaafizat
Maize	مکئی	makai
Majestic	شاندار	shaandaar
Majesty	شان	shaan
Major	اہم	ahem
Major	میجر	major
Majority	بڑا عدد	barha adad
Make	بنانا	banaana
Make	بناوٹ	banawat
Make	ساخت	saakht
Maker	بنانے والا	banaanay waala
Male	نر	nar
Malicious	بدخوا	bad-khoa
Malign	حسد	hasad

Malpractice	بدچلنی	bad-chalni
Maltreat	بدسلوکی	bad-saluki
Mamma	ماں	maa
Man	آدمی	aadmi
Man	مرد	mard
Manage	انتظام	intezaam
Management	انتظام	intezaam
Manager	منتظم	muntezam
Mandate	فرمان	farmaan
mandatory adjective	لازمی	lazmi
Mango	آم	aam
Manhood	جوانی	jawaani
Mania	جنون	junoon
Maniac	دیوانہ	diwaana
Manifest	ظاہر ہونا	zaahir hona
Manifesto noun	اعلان	elaan
Manipulate	سازباز کرنا	saazbaaz karna

Mankind	بنی آدم	bani-adam
Manly	مردانہ	mardaana
Manner	طریقہ	tareeqa
Manoeuvre	چال	chaal
Manor	حویلی	havayli
Mansion	حویلی	havayli
Manual	دستور العمل	dastoor-e-amal
Manufactory	کارخانہ	karkhaana
Manufacture	بنانا	banaana
Manure	کھاد	khaad
Many	بہت	bohot
Map	نقشہ	naqsha
Maraud	لوٹ مار کرنا	loot maar karna
Marble	سنگ مرمر	sang-e-marmar
March	آگے بڑھنا	aagay barna
March	مارچ	march
Mare noun	گھوڑی	ghoree

Marijuana	بھنگ	bhang
Marine	سمندری	samandari
Mariner	جہازی	jahaazi
Maritime	ساحلی	saahili
Mark	نشان	nishaan
Mark	ہدف	hadaf
Mark	نشان لگانا	nishaan lagaana
Mark	توجہ دینا	tawajjo dena
Market noun	بازار	baazaar
Marketing noun	مارکیٹینگ	marketing
Marksman	نشانہ بازی	nishaanaa-baaz
Maroon	عنابی رنگ	anaabi rang
Marriage	شادی	shaadi
Married	شادی شدہ	shaadi-shudaa
Marry	شادی کرنا	shaadi karna
Mars	مریغ	mir-reegh
Marsh	دلدل	daldal
Mart	دکان	dukaan

Martial	جنگی	jangi
Martyr	شہید	shaheed
Marvel	تعجب کرنا	ta'ajjub karna
Marvellous	انوکھا	anokha
Masculine	مذکر	muzakar
Mash	کچومر	kachoomar
Mask	چہرہ	chehra
Masquerade	بھیس بدلنا	bhays badalna
Mass	مادہ	maada
Mass	مواد	mavaad
Mass	ڈھیر	dhayr
Mass	عوام	awaam
Mass	عبادت کے لئے اجتماع	ibaadat kay liay ijtimaa
Massacre	قتل	qatal
Massive	وزنی	wazni
Mast	شہتیر	shehteer
Master	ماسٹر	master

Master	استاد	ustaad
Master	ماہر	maahir
Master	سربراہ	sarbaraah
Master	مہارت حاصل کرنا	mahaarat haasil karna
Masterpiece	شاہکار	shahkaar
Masticate	چبانا	chubaana
Mat	چٹائی	chataai
Match	مقابلہ	muqaabla
Match	نظیر	nazeer
Match	ماچس	maachis
Match	میچ	match
Material	سامان	samaan
Material	چیزیں	chizayn
Maternal	مادرانہ	maadaraana
Maternity	مادری رشتہ	madri rishta
Mathematics	ریاضیات	riyaaziyaat
Matrimony	شادی	shaadi

Matrix	سانچہ	saanchaa
Matron	دائی	daai
Matter	مادہ	maada
Matter	اہمیت رکھنا	ehmiyat rakhna
Matting	چٹائی	chitaai
Mattress	گدا	gadda
Mature	بالغ	baaligh
Maturity	تکمیل	takmeel
Mauve	کاسنی	kaasni
Maverick	بے مثال	bay-misaal
Maxim	قائدہ	qaa'ida
Maximum	حدغایت	had-e-ghaayat
May	مئ	mai
May	شاید	shaayed
Maybe	شاید	shaa'yed
Mayor	کوتوال	kotwaal
Maze	چکر	chakkar

Me	مجھے	mujhay
Meadow	چراگاہ	charaah-gaah
Meagre	چھوٹا	chhota
Meal	کھانا	khaana
Mean	ذلیل	zalil
Mean	درمیانی	darmiyani
Mean	اوسط	osat
Mean	معنی	maani
Mean	نیت ہونا	niyyat hona
Meander	موڑ	morh
Meaning	معنی	maa'ini
Means	ذریعے	zar-yay
Meant	مقصد تھا	maqsad tha
Meantime	اس عرصے میں	is arsay mein
Meanwhile	جس دوران	jis doraan
Measure	ناپنا	naapna
Measure	پیمائش کرنا	paymaish karna

Measure	ناپ	naap
Measure	پیمائش	paymaish
Measurement	ناپ	naap
Meat	گوشت	gosht
Mechanic	دستکار	dastkaar
Mechanical	مشین کا	machine ka
Medal	تمغہ	tamgha
Meddle	دخل دینا	dakhal dayna
Mediate	بیچ بچاؤ کرنا	beech bachao karna
Mediation	شفاعت	shifaa'at
Mediator	صالص	saalis
Medical	طبی	tibbi
Medicine	دوا	dawa
Mediocre	درمیانہ	darmiyaana
Meditation	غور	ghor
Medium	درمیانہ	darmiyaana
Meet	ملنا	milna
Meet	ملاقات کرنا	mulaqat karna

Meeting	ملاقات	mulaaqaat
Megan	میگن	megan
noun		
mehnaz noun; name	مہناز	mehnaz
mehvish noun; name of a girl	محوش	mehvish
Melancholy	افسردگی	afsurdgi
Melody	سر	sur
Melody	آہنگ	aahang
MELON noun; fruit	خربوزہ	kharbooza
Melt	پگھلنا	pighlaana
Member	ممبر	member
Membrane	پردہ	parda
Memento	نشانی	nishani
Memoir	تذکرہ	tazkira
Memorable	یادگار	yaadgaar
Memorandum	دستاویز	dastawaiz
Memorial	یادگار	yaadgaar
Memory	یاداشت	yadasht

Men	مرد	mard
Men	آدمی	aadmi
Menace	دھمکی	dhamki
Mend	مرمت کرنا	murammat karna
Menial	ادنہ	adna
Mensuration	ناپ	naap
Mental	دماغی	damaaghi
Mention	ذکر کرنا	zikar karna
Menu Noun	فہرست طعام	fihrist taam
Merchandise	سودا	soda
Merchandize	سودا	soda
Merchant	سوداگر	sodaagar
Merciful	کریم	kareem
Merciless	سنگدل	sangdil
Mercury	عطارد	ataarad
Mercy	رحم	rehem
Mere	محض	mehez

Merely	صرف	sirf
Merge	مل جانا	mil jana
Merit	خوبی	khubi
Merry	زندہدل	zinda dil
Mesh	جالی	jaali
Mess	ستیاناس	satyaanaas
Message	پیغام	peghaam
Messenger	پیغمبر	peghambar
Messenger	پیغامبر	peghaambar
Metal	دھات	dhaat
Metaphor	تسبیح	tashbih
Meteor	شہاب ثاقب	shahaab-e-saaqib
Meteorite	شہاب ثاقب	shahaab-e-saaqib
Method	طریقہ	tareeqa
Microscope	خردبین	khurdbeen
Mid	درمیانی	darmiyaani
Midday	دوپہر	dupeher

Middle	درمیان	darmiyaan
Middle	وسط	wast
Middle noun	درمیان	darmiyaan
Middle	وسطی	wasti
Midnight	آدھی رات	aadhi raat
Midst	بیچ	beech
Might	شاید	shaayed
Might	زور	zor
Might	طاقت	taaqat
Mighty	طاقتور	taaqatwar
Migrate	ہجرت کرنا	hijrat karna
Migration	ہجرت	hijrat
Mild	ہلکا	halka
Mile	میل	meel
Military	اسکری	askari
Milk	دودھ	doodh
Mill	چکی	chakki
Million	دس لاکھ	das lakh

Minaret	منار	minaar
Mince	قیمہ	qeema
Mind	دماغ	dimaagh
Mind	ذہن	zehn
Mind	دھیان دینا	dhiyan dena
Mind	یاد رکھنا	yaad rakhna
Mine	میرا	mayra
Mineral	معدنی	maa'dani
Mineralogy	علم معدنیات	ilm-e-madniyaat
Mingle	ملانا	milaana
Miniature	چھوٹی	chhoti
Minimum	قلیل	qaleel
Minister	وزیر	wazeer
Ministry	وزارت	wazaarat
Minnow	دریائی مچھلی	daryaai machhli
Minor	چھوٹا	chhota
Minority	اقلیت	aqliyat
Mint	پودینہ	podina

Minus	منفی	manfi
Minute	منٹ	minute
Minute	باریک	bareek
Minute	خفیف	khafif
Miracle	معجزہ	mojza
Miraculous	حیرت انگیز	hairat angez
Mirage	سراب	saraab
Mirror	آئینہ	aaina
Mirth	خوشی	khushi
Misadventure	بدقسمتی	bad-qismati
Misapply	بے جا استعمال	bayjaa-istaymaal
Misapprehend	غلط سمجھنا	ghalat samajhna
Misapprehension	غلط فہمی	ghalat-fehmi
Misbehave	بدتمیزی کرنا	bad-tameezi karna
Misbehaviour	بدسلوکی	bad-salooki
Miscalculate	غلط اندازہ	ghalat-andaaza

Miscarriage	اسقاط حمل	isqaat-e-hamal
Miscellaneous	مختلف	mukhtalif
Mischance	کم بختی	kam-bakhti
Mischief	شرارت	sharaarat
Mischievous	شرارتی	sharaarti
Miser	کنجوس	kanjoos
Miserable	ناخوش	na khush
Misery	تکلیف	takleef
Misinform	غلط خبر دینا	ghalat khabar dena
Misinterpretation	غلط معنی	ghalat maa'ni
Mislead	دھوکا	dhoka dena
Misplace	بے ٹھکانے ہونا	bay-thikaanay hona
Misprint	غلط چھاپنا	ghalat chhaapna
Mispronounce	غلط تلفظ کرنا	ghalat talaffuz karna
Misreport	غلط بیانی	ghalat biyaani
Misrule	بدانتظامی	bad-intezami
Miss	مس	miss

Miss	خطا ہونا	khata hona
Miss	کھو دینا	kho dena
Miss	کمی محسوس کرنا	kami mehsoos karna
Missile	مزائیل	missile
Missing	گم	gum
Mission	مہم	muhim
Missionary	مبلغ دین	muballigh-e-din
Misspell	غلط ہجے کرنا	ghalat hijay karna
Misspend	بیجا صرف کرنا	beja sarf karna
Misstate	غلط بیان کرنا	ghalat biyaan karna
Mist	دھند	dhund
Mistake	غلطی	ghalti
Mix	ملانا	milaana
Mix	آمیزش کرنا	aamayzish karna
Mobile noun; wireless	موبائل	mobile
model noun	ماڈل	model
Moderate	معتدل	mo'tadil

Modern	جدید	jadeed
Molecule	سالمہ	saalma
Mom	امی	ammi
Moment	لمحہ	lamhaa
Monday	پیر	peer
Money	روپیہ پیسہ	ropya paysa
Money	رقم	raqam
Monkey	بندر	bandar
Month	مہینہ	mahina
Moon	چاند	chand
moral adjective	اخلاقی	akhlaqi
More	اور	aur
More	زیادہ	ziyada
Morning noun	صبح	subaah
Morning	سویرا	sawayra
moron noun	احمق	ehmaq
Mosque	مسجد	masjid

Most	اکثر	aksar
Most	سب سے زیادہ	sab say ziyada
Mother	ماں	maan
Mother	امی	ammi
Mother	والدہ	walda
Motion	حرکت	harkat
Motion	درخواست	darkhaast
motivation an incentive for action	ترغیب سبب	targheeb sabab
Mount	سوار ہونا	sawaar hona
Mount	چڑھانا	charhhana
Mountain	پہاڑ	pahaarh
mouse noun	چوہا	chu-waah
Mouth	منہ	muhn
Move	حرکت کرنا	harkat karna
Move	ہلانا	hilaana
Move	دھکیلنا	dhakaylna
movement noun	جدوجہد	jidojehed

Movie noun	فلم	film
Much	کافی سارا	kafi saara
Muhammad noun; male name	محمد	Muhammad
Multiply	ضرب دینا	zarb dayna
Multiply	تعداد بڑھانا	taadad barhhaana
Multitude	کثرت	kasrat
Mum	ماں	maa
Mumble	بڑبڑانا	burhburhaana
Munch	چبانا	chubaana
Municipal	شہری	shehri
Murder	قتل کرنا	qatal karna
Murder noun	قتل	qatal
Murderer	قاتل	qaatil
Murky	دھندھلا	dhundhla
Murmur	بربرانا	burburaahat
Museum	عجائب گھر	ajaaib ghar

Musician	سازنواز	saaz-nawaaz
Muslim noun	مسلم	muslim
muslim noun	مسلمان	musalmaan
Must	لازمی	lazmi
Mustafa noun	مصطفی	mustafa
mustard noun	سرسؤں	sarson
Mute	آواز دبانا	awaaz-dabaana
Mutinous	مفسد	mufsid
Mutiny	بغاوت	baghaawat
Mutual adjective	باہمی	bahami
My	میرا	mayra
Myself	میں خود	mein khud
Mysterious	پراسرار	pur-asraar
Mystic adjective	صوفیانہ	sufiaana
Mystic noun	صوفی	sufi
Mystify	پیشیدہ	paysheeda
Myth	داستان	daastaan

N – O – P

Nail	ناخن	naakhun
Nail	کیل	keel
Naive	بھولا بھالا	bhola bhaala
naked adjective	ننگا	nanga
Name	نام رکھنا	naam rakhna
Name	نام	naam
Nap	آنک لگنا	aankh lagna
Narrow	تنگ	tang
Nation	قوم	qaum
National	قومی	qaumi
Nationality	وطنیت	watniyat
Native	مقامی	maqaami
Natural	قدرتی	qudrati
Nature	قدرت	qudrat
Nature	فطرت	fitrat
Naughty	شرارتی	sharaarti

Navigate	جہاز رانی کرنا	jahaaz-raani karna
Navigation	جہاز رانی	jahaaz-raani
Near	نزدیک	nazdik
Near	قریب	qarib
Near	نزدیکی	nazdeeki
Neat	صاف	saaf
Necessary	ضروری	zaroori
Neck	گردن	gardan
Necklace	ہار	haar
Need	ضرورت	zaroorat
Need	ضرورت ہونا	zaroorat hona
Needle	سوئی	sui
Negative	منفی	manfi
Neglect	نظرانداز کرنا	nazar andaaz karna
negotiate baat cheet karna	باتچیت کرنا	baat cheet karna
Neighbor	پڑوسی	parhosi
Neighbour	پڑوسی	parosee
Neither	نہ یہ نہ وہ	na-yeh na-woh

Nephew	بھتیجا	bhateeja
Neptune	نیپٹیون	neptune
Nero	ظالم	zaalim
Nerve	رگ	rag
Nervous	پریشان	pareshaan
Nervousness	پریشانی	parayshaani
Nest	گھونسلا	ghonsla
Net	قل	qul (resultant)
Neural	عصبی	asbi
Neutral	غیرجانبدار	ghayr-jaanibdaar
Never	کبھی نہیں	kabhi nahin
Nevertheless	بہرحال	beher-haal
New	نیا	nya
News	خبریں	khabarain
Newspaper	اخبار	akhbaar
Next	اگلا	aglaa
Next	بعد کا	baad ka
Nexus	تعلق	taa'luq

Nib	چونچ	chonch
Nibble	کترنا	kutarna
Nice	اچھا	achcha
niece noun	بھتیجی	bhateeji
Night	رات	raat
Nightingale	بلبل	bulbul
Nightmare	ڈراؤنا خواب	draaona khuaab
Nincumpoop noun; a naive person	بدھو	buddhoo
Nine	نو	nau
Nineteen	انیس	un-nees
Ninety	نوے	nawway
Nipple	چوسنی	chusni
No	نہیں	nahin
Noble adjective	نجیب	najeeb
Nod	سر ہلانا	sar hilaana
Noise	شور	shor
None	کوئی نہیں	koi nahin
nonsense noun	فضول	fazul

Noon	دوپہر	do peher
nope adverb	نہیں	nahee
Nor	نہیں	nahin
Nor	نہ	nah
normal adjective	معامولی	maamooli
North	شمال	shumal
Northern	شمالی	shumaali
Nose	ناک	naak
Not	نہیں	naheen
Notable	قابل توجہ	qaabil-e-tawajjo
Notch	نشان	nishaan
Note	نوٹ	note
Note	یاداشت	yaa-daasht
Nothing	کچھ نہیں	kuchh nahin
Notice	نوٹس	notice
Notice	اطلاع	ittela
Notice	اعلان	elaan
Notify	خبردینا	khabar dena

Notion	خیال	khiyaal
Notorious	بدنام	bad-naam
Noun	اسم	ism
Nourish	پرورش کرنا	parwarish karna
Nourishment	غذا	ghaza
Novel	ناول	novel
Novelist	ناول نگار	novel-nigaar
Novelty	انوکھی	anokhi
November	نومبر	november
Novice	مبتری	mubtari
Now	ابھی	abhi
Now	اب	ab
Nowadays	آج کل	aaj kal
Nuclear	نیوکلیائی	nucli'aai
Nude	ننگا	nanga
Nudge	کہنی دینا	kohni dena
Numb	سن ہوجانا	sun ho jaana
Number	نمبر	number

Number	ہندسہ	hindsa
Number	عدد	adad
Numeral	عددی	adadi
Nurse	نرس	nurse
nutmeg noun; fruit	جئےفل	jaye fal
Oak	شاہ بلوط	shah-baloot
Oar	چپو	chappu
Oasis	نخلستان	nakhlistan
Oath	عہد	ehed
oatmeal noun; oatmeal	جای کا آٹا	jaee ka aata
Obedience	تعبداری	taa'bedari
Obedient	تابعدار	tabedaar
Obesity Overweight	موٹاپا	motaapaa
Obey	حکم ماننا	hukam manaana
Obituary	موتکی خبر	mot ki khabar
Object	شے	shay
Object	چیز	cheez
Object	مقصد	maqsad

Object	موضوع	mozoo
Object	اعتراض کرنا	etaraaz karna
Objection	اعتراض	ay'tayraaz
objective noun	مقصد	maqsad
Obligation	ذمہ داری	zimedaari
Obligatory	لازمی	laazmi
Oblige	راضی کرنا	razi karna
Obliterate	مٹانا	mitaana
Oblivion	بھول	bhool
Oblivious	غافل	ghaafil
Obnoxious	ناقبل برداشت	naa-qabil-e- bardaasht
Obscenity noun	فحاشی	fahaashi
Obscure	مبہم	mub-ham
Observant	پابند	paa-band
Observe	مشاہدہ کرنا	mushaahida karna
Observe	بیان کرنا	bayaan karna
obsess verb	وہم کرنا	wehem karna
Obsessed adjective	وہمی	wahemi

Obstacle	رکاوٹ	rukaawat
Obstinate	ضدی	ziddi
Obtain	حاصل کرنا	haasil karna
Obvious	صاف ظاہر	saaf zaahir
Occasion	موقع	moqaa
Occupation	پیشہ	paysha
Occupy	قبضہ کرنا	qabza karna
Occur	پیش آنا	paysh aana
Occur	واقع ہونا	waaqay hona
Occur	خیال آنا	khayaal aana
Oceam	سمندر	samandar
Ocean	بحر	beher
October	اکتوبر	october
Odd adjective	عجیب	ajeeb
Odour	بو	boo
Of	کا	ka
Of	تعلق	taalluq
Off	دور	dur

Off	الگ	alag
Offence	جرم	jurm
Offer	پیشکش	payshkash
Offer	پیش کرنا	paysh karnaa
Office	آفس	office
Office	دفتر	dafter
Office	عہدہ	ohdaa
Official	سرکاری	sarkaari
Often	اکثر	aksar
Oh	اوہ	oh
Oh	اف	oof
Oil	تیل	tayl
Oil	تیل ملنا	tayl malnaa
Ointment	مرہم	marham
Ok	ٹھیک ہے	theek hay
Okay	ٹھیک ہے	theek hay
okra noun	بھنڈی	bhindi
Old	پرانا	puraana

Old	بوڑھا	boorhhaa
Old	قدیم	qadeem
Olive noun	زیتون	zaitoon
Omen noun	شگون	Shagoon
On	جاری	jaari
On	پر	per
On	اوپر	ooper
Once	ایک دفعہ	ek dafaa
One	ایک	ek
Onion	پیاز	pyaaz
Only	اکیلا	akaylaa
Only	اکلوتا	aklotaa
Only	البتہ	albattaa
Open	کھولنا	kholna
Open	کھلا ہوا	khulaa hua
Operate	کام کرنا	kaam karnaa
Operate	عمل کرنا	amal karnaa
Operate	چلانا	chalaana

Operation	کام	kaam
Opinion	رائے	raa-ay
Opportunity noun	موقع	moqah
Oppose verb	مخالفت کرنا	Mukhaalifat karna
Oppose verb	مخالفت کرنا	mukhaalifat karnaa
Opposite	مخالف	mukhaalif
Opposite	مقابل	muqaabil
Opposite	متضاد	mutazaad
Oppression	زبردستی	zabar-dasti
optimistic adjective	امید پسند	umeed pasand
option adjective	اختیار	ikhtiar
Or	یا	yaa
Orange	نارنجی	naaranji
Orbit	مدار	madaar
Order	حکم	hukm
Order	حکم دینا	hukm dayna
Order	ضابطہ	zaabtaa
Order noun	فرمان	farmaan

Ordinary	عام	aam
Organ	آلہ	aala
Organ	ساز	saaz
organism noun; bird	جاندار	jaan daar
Organization	ادارہ	idaara
Organize	ترتیب دینا	tarteeb dayna
Original	اصلی	asli
Orphan	یتیم	yateem
Ostrich	شترمرغ	shatar-murgh
Other	دوسرا	doosra
Other	دیگر	digar
Other adj	دیگر	deegar
Our	ہمارا	hamaaraa
Out	باہر	baahir
Out	بجھا ہوا	bujha hua
Outside	باہر	baahir
Over	اوپر	ooper
Over	ختم ہونا	khatam hona

Overturn	الٹنا	ulatna
Owe	مقروض ہونا	maqruz hona
Owl	الو	ullu
Own	اپنا	apnaa
Own	اپنانا	apnaanaa
Own	مالک ہونا	maalik hona
Oxygen	آکسیجن	oxygen
Pace	رفتار	raftaar
Pacific	کاہل	kaahil
Pacify	امن قائم کرنا	aman qaa'em karna
Pack	باندھنا	baandhna
Package	پیکج	package
Packet	لفافہ	packet
Pact	عہد	ehed
Paddle	چپو	chappu
Page	صفحہ	safha
Pail	بالٹی	baalti
Pain	تکلیف	takleef

Paint	رنگ	rang
Pair	جوڑا	jora
Pakistan	پاکستان	pakistan
pakistani noun	پاکستانی	pakistani
palace noun	محل	mahal
Pale	ہلکا	halka
Palm	ہتھیلی	hathayli
Pancreas noun	تلی	Tilli
Panic	پریشانی	parayshaani
Pant	ہانپنا	haanpna
Paper	کاغذ	kaaghaz
Paradise	جنت	jannat
Pardon	معافی	maafi
Parent noun; mother	ماں	maa
Parent noun; father	باپ	baap
parrot noun	طوطا	tota
parsley noun	اجوان کا پتہ	ajwain ka patta
Part	جز	juz

Particle	ذره	zarra
Particular	خصوصی	khasoosi
partition noun	تقسیم	taqseem
Partner	ساتھی	saath
Party	دعوت	dawat
Pass	گزرنا	guzarna
Passage	راستہ	rasta
Passion	جذبہ	jazba
Passionate	پرجوش	purjosh
Past	ماضی	maazi
Paste verb	چپکانا	chapkaanaa
Pat	تھپکی دینا	thapki dena
Patch	پیوند	paywand
Path	راستہ	rasta
pathetic adjective	رقت انگیز	riqqat angez
Patience	صبر	sabr
Patient	مریض	mareez
Patriot noun	محب وطن	Muhib-e-watan

Pattern	نمونہ	namoona
Pause	وقفہ	waqfa
Pay	ادا کرنا	ada karna
Peace	امن	aman
peaceful adjective	پرامن	pur-aman
Peach	آڑو	aarhu
peacock in a zoo	مور	mowr
Peak	چوٹی	choti
pear noun	ناشپاتی	naashpaati
Pearl	موتی	moti
peas vegetable	مٹر	muttor
Pee noun	پیشاب	peeshab
Pen	قلم	qalm
Pen noun; fenced enclosure	احاطہ	Ahaata
Penalty	جرمانہ	jurmana
Pending adjective; waiting for	زیر غور	zer-e-goor
penis noun; male organ	عضو تناسل	uzu-i-tanasul

People	لوگ	log
Pepper	مرچ	mirch
Percentage	فیصد	feesad
perception noun	شعور	shaoor
Perfect adjective	بہترین	behtareen
Perform	انجام دینا	anjaam dayna
performance noun	کارکردگی	kaarkardagi
Perfume	خوشبو	khushboo
Perhaps	شاید	shaa'id
Period noun	دور	dor
Perish	فنا ہونا	fanaa hona
Permission	اجازت	ijazat
Permit	اجازت دینا	ijazat dayna
Persist	اصرار کرنا	israr karna
Person	انسان	insaan
personal adjective	اپنی	aapni
Personality noun	شخصیت	shakhseeyat
Persuade	راضی کرنا	razi karna

pervaiz noun; name	پرویز	pervaiz
Pet	پالتو	paaltoo
Philosopher	فلسفی	falsafi
Philosophy	فلسفہ	falsafa
Phone noun	فون	phone
Photograph	تصویر	tasveer
Physician	طبیب	tabeeb
Physics	طبیعیات	tab'iyat
Piano	پیانو	piano
Pick	چننا	chunna
Picture	تصویر	tasweer
Piece	ٹکڑا	tukra
Pierce	چیدنا	cheedna
Pig	سؤر	suar
Pigeon	کبوتر	kabutar
Pillow noun	تکیہ	Takyah
pineapple noun; fruit	انناس	ananas
Pink	گلابی	gulabi

Pinnacle	چوٹی	choti
Piss verb	پیشاب کرنا	peshab karna
Pistol	پستول	pistol
Pit	گڑھا	garh'ha
Place	جگہ	jagaa
Placid	پرسکون	pur-sakoon
Plain	ہموار	hamvar
Plan	منصوبہ	mansooba
Plane	ہوائی جہاز	hawai jahaz
Plant	پودا	poda
Plastic	پلاسٹک	plastic
plate noun	تھالی	thali
Platitude	عام بات	aam baat
Play	کھیلنا	khelna
Player	کھلاڑی	khilaari
Please	خوش کرنا	khush karna
Pleasure	فرحت	farhat
Pledge verb	وعدہ کرنا	Wadah karna

Pluck	اکھاڑنا	ukharna
Plum	آلوبخارا	aalu bukhara
Plumber	سیسہ گر	seesa-gar
Plunder verb	غارت	ghaarat
Pluto	پلوٹو	pluto
Pocket	جیب	jayb
Poem	نظم	nazm
Poet	شاعر	shaa'ir
Poetry	شاعری	shairi
point noun	نقطہ	nuqta
Poison	زہر	zeher
Poke	گھسیڑنا	ghuserna
police noun	پولیس	police
Policy	طریقہ کار	tareeka-e-kaar
polite adjective	شائستہ	shaysta
Politics	سیاست	siyaasat
Pomegranate noun; anar	انار	Anar
Poor	غریب	gareeb
Pope	پاپائےروم	paapaa-e-rome

Popular	مشہور	mashhur
Populated adjective	آباد	aabaad
Population	آبادی	abaadi
Porcupine noun	ژوژ	zhuzh
Pork	لحم خنزیر	laham-e-khinzeer
Porn noun	فحش	fahsh
Position noun	جگہ	Jagah
Positive	صحیح	sahih
Possession	ملکیت	milkiyyat
Possible	ممکن	mumkin
Post	بھجوانا	bhijwaanaa
Post	خطوط	khatoot
Post	کھمبا	khambaa
Postpone	ملتوی کرنا	multavi karna
Potato	آلو	alu
Potent	طاقتور	taqat-war
Potentate	حاکم	haakim
Potential	قابلیت	qaabliyyat

poverty noun	غربت	ghurbat
Powder	برادہ	buraada
Power	طاقت	taaqat
Powerful adjective	طاقت ور	taaqatwar
Practical	عملی	amli
practice noun; typical action	معمول	mamool
practice noun	مشق	mashk
Practician	پیشاوار	pesha-war
Praise	تعریف	ta'reef
Pray	عبادت کرنا	ibadat karna
Prayer	دعا	dua
Prayer noun	نماز	namaaz
Pre	قبل	qabl
Precious	قیمتی	qeemti
Precise	صحیح	sahih
Predict	پیشگوئی کرنا	pesh-goi karna
Prefer	ترجیح دینا	tarjeeh dena
Pregnant noun; pregnant woman	حاملۂ	hamela

Prejudice Noun	تعصب	Taasub
Premise	احاطہ	ihata
Premises	احاطے	ihatay
Prepare	تیار کرنا	tayyar karna
presence noun	موجودگی	maujudagi
Present	پیش کرنا	paish karna
president noun	صدر	sadr
Pressure	دباؤ	dabao
Prestige	شہرت	shohrat
pretend verb	ظاہر کرنا	zahir karna
pretend verb	بننا	banna
Pretty	پیارا	piyara
Prevent verb	روکنا	roknaa
Previous	پچھلا	pitchlaa
Prey	شکار	shikar
Price	قیمت	qeemat
Pride	غرور	gharoor

Primitive	ابتدائی	ibtedai
Prince	شہزادہ	shehzada
Princely	شاہانہ	shahana
Princess	شہزادی	shehzadi
Principal	بڑا	barha
Principle	اصول	asool
Print	چھاپنا	chapna
Prior	قبل	qabal
Priority noun	ترجیح	tarjeeh
Prison	قیدخانہ	qed-khana
Privacy	پوشیدگی	posheedgi
Private	ذاتی	zaati
Privilege	استحقاق	istehkak
Prize	انعام	inaam
probably adverb	غالباً	ghaalban
Problem noun	مسلہ	masla
Process noun	عمل	amal
procurement noun	حصول	hasool
Produce	پیدا کرنا	peda karna

Product	پیداوار	pedawar
Production	پیداوار	pedawar
Profession	پیشہ	paysha
Professional	پیشہ ور	payshawar
Profit	منافع	munaafa
Progress noun	ترقّی	taraqqi
project noun	منصو بہ	mansoba
Prominent adjective	نمایاں	numaya
Promise	وعدہ	wada
Promising	امیدافزا	umid-afza
Promote	بڑھانا	barhaana
Promotion	ترقی	taraqi
Pronunciation	تلفظ	talafuz
Proof	ثبوت	suboot
proper adjective	سیدھا	sidha
property noun	املاک	amlaak
property noun	جائیداد	jaedaad
prophet noun	رسول	rasool

prosperity noun	کامیابی	kamyabi
prosperous adjective	خوشحال	khushhaal
Prostitute noun; impolite	ر نڈ ی	randi
Protect	حفاظت کرنا	hifazat karna
Protection	حفاظت	hifaazat
Protest	احتجاج کرنا	ehtejaj karna
Protocol	رسوم	rasoom
proud adjective	فاخر	faakhir
Prove	ثابت کرنا	sabit karna
Provide	مہیہ کرنا	muhayya karna
Province	صوبہ	subah
Provincial	صوبائی	subaai
Provocation	اشتعال	ishtial
Provocative	اکسانے والا	uksanay wala
Prune	تراشنا	tarashna
public noun	عوام	awam
Pull	کھینچنا	khaynchnaa
Pumpkin kadoo	کددو	kadoo

Punish	سزا دینا	saza dayna
punishment noun	سزا	suza
Purchase	خریدنا	khareedna
pure adjective	خالص	khaalis
Purification	صفائی	safai
Purify	صاف کرنا	saaf karna
Purity	پاکیزگی	pakeezgi
Purple noun	جامنی	jamani
Purpose	مقصد	maqsad
Pursue	پیچھا کرنا	peechha karna
Push	دھکا دینا	dhakka dena
Put	رکھنا	rakhna

Q – R

Qualification	قابلیت	qabliyat
Quality	کیفیت	kefiyat
Quantity	مقدار	miqdar
Quarantine	قرنطینہ	qarantina
Quarrel	جھگڑا کرنا	jhagra karna
Quarter	چوتھائی	chothaai
Queen	ملکہ	malka
Queer	عجیب	ajeeb
Quench	بجھانا	bujhana
Quest	تلاش	talash
Question	سوال	sawaal
Queue	قطار	qataar
Quick	جلدی	jaldi
Quiet	خاموش	khamosh
Quit	چھوڑنا	chhorhnaa
Quite	قطعی	qatai

Quiver	تھرتھرانا	thartharana
quote noun; reference of a word or passage	حوالہ دینا	hawala dena
quote verb; name a price	بولی لگانا	boli lagana
Rabbit	خرگوش	khargosh
Race	دوڑ	dorh
Rachel	ریچل	rachel
Racket	ہنگامہ	hangama
Rage	غصہ	gussa
Rain	بارش	barish
Raise	بلند کرنا	buland karna
Raja	راجہ	raja
Rally	مظاہرہ	muzahira
random noun	بےترتیب	bay-tarteeb
Range	پہنچ	pohanch
Rap	کھٹکھٹانا	khatkhatana
Rape sexual assault	زنا بالجبر	zana-bil-jabar
Rapid	تیز	tez

Rare	نایاب	nayaab
rather verb	ترجیح کرنا	tarjeeh karna
rational adjective	عاقل	aaqil
Raw	کچا	kacha
Ray	کرن	kiran
Reach	پہنچنا	pahonchna
Reaction	ردعمل	rad-e-amal
Read	پڑھنا	parhna
Ready	تیار	tayyar
Real	اصلی	asli
Reality	حقیقت	haqiqat
Realize	احساس کرنا	ayh-saas karnaa
Really	اصل میں	asal mein
Realm	سلطنت	saltanat
Rear	پچھلا	pichla
Reason	وجہ	wajah
Rebate	کمی	kammi

rebellion noun	بھگاوت	bhagaavat
Recall	یاد کرنا	yaad karna
Receive	وصول کرنا	wasool karna
Recent	حالیہ	halia
recession noun	ما لیاتی بہران	maliati bohran
Recipe	ترکیب	tarkeeb
Recite verb	تلاوت	Telawat
Recognize	پہچاننا	pehchanna
Recommend	تعریف کرنا	tareef karna
reconcile verb	مصالحت کرنا	musaalihat karna
Record	ریکارڈ	record
recruit noun	نئی بھرتی	nae bharti
Red	لال	laal
Red noun	سرخ	surkh
Reduce	کم کرنا	kam karna
Reference	توسط	tavassut
Refine	صاف کرنا	saaf karna

Reflect	منعکس کرنا	munakis karna
Reflection	عکس	aks
Refresh	تازہ دم ہونا	taza dam hona
Refuge	پناہ	panaah
Refurbish	پھرچمکانا	phir chamkana
Refuse	انکار کرنا	inkar karna
regarding preposition	بابت	babat
regardless adverb	قطع نظر	kataa-nazar
regards injection	آداب	adaab
Region noun	علاقہ	ilaaqah
Regret	پشیمان	pasheman karna
regular adjective	باقاعدگی سے	regular
Reinstate verb	بحال کرنا	bahaal karna
reject verb	مسترد کرنا	mustarad karna
Rejoice	خوش ہونا	khush hona
Relate	رابطہ قائم کرنا	rabta qaim karna
Related	تعلق رکھنا	taluq rakhna

Relation	تعلق	taluq
Relationship	تعلق	ta'luq
relative noun	رشتہ دار	rishtedaar
Relax	آرام کرنا	araam karna
Relaxation	آرام	araam
Release	رہا کرنا	riha karna
Reliable	قابل اعتماد	qabil-e-etemad
Relief	آرام	araam
Religion	مذہب	mazhab
Religion noun	دین	deen
Religious	مذہبی	mazhabi
Reluctance	ہچکچاہٹ	hichkichahat
Rely	بھروسا کرنا	bharosa karna
Remain	رہنے والا	rehne wala
Remainder	بقیہ	baqiyah
Remedy	علاج	ilaaj
Remember	یاد رکھنا	yaad rakhna
Remind	یاد دلانا	yaad dilana

Remote	دور دراز	dur daraz
Remove	ہٹانا	hatana
Renounce	چھوڑنا	chhorna
renounce verb	منسوخ	mansookh
Rep	نمائندہ	numainda
Repair	مرمت کرنا	murammat karna
Repeat	دہرانا	duhrana
Reply	جواب دینا	jawab dena
republic noun	جمہوریت	jamhuriat
Reputation	شہرت	shohrat
Request	درخواست کرنا	darkhaast karna
required adverb	درکار	darkaar
Rescue	بچانا	bachana
Research	تفتیش	taftish
Reservoir	ذخیرہ	zakheera
Resist	روکنا	rokna
Resistance	مقابلہ	muqaabala

resolution noun	قرارداد	qaraardaad
Resource	وسیلہ	waseela
Resources	وسائل	wasail
Respect	عزت کرنا	izzat karna
Respect adjective	اخلاق	akhlaaq
Respectable adjective	محترم	muhtaram
Respond	جواب دینا	jawaab dena
Response	جواب	jawab
Rest	آرام کرنا	araam karna
Restaurant	ریسٹورانٹ	restaurant
restriction noun	پابندی	pabandi
Result	نتیجہ	nateeja
resume verb	دوبارہ شروع کرنا	dobara shroo karna
retain verb	رکھنا	rakhnaa
retained noun	رکھا ہوا	rakhaa hua
Retreat	پیچھے ہٹنا	peechay hatna
Return	واپس کرنا	wapas karna

Reveal	ظاہر کرنا	zahir karna
Revenge	بدلہ	badla
revenge noun	انتقام	inteqaam
Revision	تبدیلی	tabdeeli
Revival	بحالی	behaali
Revoke	منسوخ کرنا	mansookh karna
Revolution	انقلاب	inqalab
Reward	انعام	inaam
Rice	چاول	chawal
Rich	امیر	ameer
Riddle	پہیلی	paheli
Ride	سواری	sawari
Ridicule	مضحکہ کرنا	muzehka karna
Ridiculous	مضحکہ خیز	muzehka khez
Right	دائیں	daain
Right	حق	haq
Rigorous	شدید	shadeed

ring noun; a characteristic sound	بجنا	bajna
ring noun; jewelry	انگوٹھی	angoothi
Riot	جھگڑ	jhagar
rise verb; to move upward	اٹھنا	uthna
risk noun	خطرہ	khatraa
Ritual Noun	رسم	Rasm
Rival	مخالف	mukhalif
Rivalry	رقابت	raqaabat
River	دریا	darya
Road	سڑک	sarhak
Rob	لوٹ لینا	lut lena
Rock noun	پتھر	patthar
role verb	کردار ادا کرنا	kirdaar adaa karnaa
Romance noun	عشق	ishq
Romantic adjective	رومانوی	Romaanvi
Roof noun	چھت	chhat
Room	کمرہ	kamra

Rope	رسی	rassi
Rose	گلاب	gulaab
rot verb	سڑنا	sarkhnaa
Royal	شاہانہ	shaahaanaa
Rub	رگڑنا	ragarhna
Rubbish	کچرا	kachra
Rude	بدتمیز	bad-tameez
Ruin	تباہ کرنا	tabah karna
Rule noun (law)	اصول	usool
Rule noun	حکومت	hakoomat
Rumour	افواہ	afwa
Run	بھاگنا	bhagna
Rush noun	جلدی	jaldi
Russia	روس	roos
Rust	زنگ	zang

S

Sack	بوری	bori
Sacred	مقدس	muqaddas
sacrifice noun	قربانی	qurbaani
Sad	اداس	udaas
Safe	محفوظ	mehfooz
Safeguard	حفاظت کرنا	hifazat karna
safety noun	حفاظت	hifaazat
safiya noun; name	صفیا	safiya
Said verb	کہا	kaha
Sail	بہری سفر کرنا	behri safar karna
Sake	خاطر	khaatir
salam noun	سالم	salam
Salary	تنخواہ	tankhua
Salient	نمایاں	numaya
salman noun; male name	سلمان	salman
Salt	نمک	namak

Same	یکسان	yaksaan
Sample	نمونہ	namoona
sana noun; name	ثنا	sana
sana noun; name; alternate spelling	ثناء	sana
Sand	ریت	rayt
sapphire noun	نیلم	neelam
Sarah noun	سارہ	sarah
Sarcastic adjective	طعن آمیز	tan-amayz
Satisfaction	اطمینان	itminan
Satisfy	تسلی کرنا	tasali karna
Saturday	ہفتہ	hafta
Save	بچانا	bachana
Savoury adjective	مزے دار	mazedaar
Saw	آری	aari
Say	کہنا	kehna
scam noun	دھوکا	dhoka
Scan	غور سے دیکھنا	ghor se dekhna

Scarce	قلیل	qaleel
Scarcity	کمی	kami
Scare	ڈرانا	darana
Scarf noun	دوپٹہ	dupatta
Scary	ڈراؤنا	dharaaona
Scatter	پھیلانا	phelana
Scenario noun	منظر نامہ	Manzer Naama
Scene	منظر	manzar
Scent	خوشبو	khushboo
School	مدرسہ	madarassa
Science	سائینس	science
Scientist	سائینس دان	science-daan
Scissors	قینچی	qainchi
Scold	ڈانٹنا	dantna
scope noun	گنجائش	gunjaish
Scorn	حقارت	haqarat
Scramble	الٹ پلٹ کرنا	ulat-pulat karna

Scream	چلانا	chilana
Screwdriver noun	پیچ کس	Paich Kass
Script	تحریر	tehreer
Scroll	لپیٹنا	lapetna
Scrutiny	نجس	najas
Sea	سمندر	samandar
Search	تلاش کرنا	talash karna
Search verb	کھوج	khoj
Season	موسم	mosam
Seat	نشست	nashist
Secede verb	قطع تعلق کرنا	qata tayaluq karna
Seclude	الگ رکھنا	alag rakhna
Second adjective	دوسرا	doosra
Secret	راز	raaz
Section	حصہ	hissa
Secure	محفوظ	mehfooz
Security	حفاظت	hifaazat
See	دیکھنا	dekhna

Seed	بیج	beej
Seek	تلاش	talash
seem verb	لگنا	lagna
Seen	دیکھا	daykha
Seize	پکڑنا	pakarna
Seldom	کبھی کبھار	kabhi kabhar
Select	چننا	chunna
Self	خود	khud
Selfish	خود غرض	khudgarz
Sell	بیچنا	bechna
semen noun	منی	mani
Send	بھیجنا	bhejna
Sense	شعور	sha'oor
Sensitive	حساس	hasaas
Sentence	جملہ	jumla
Sentence	سزا	saza
Separate	علیحدہ	alehda

separation noun	علیحدگی	alaydgi
September	ستمبر	september
sequence noun	ترتیب	tarteeb war
Serious	سنجیدہ	sanjeeda
Seriously	سنجیدگی سے	sanjidgi se
Servant	نوکر	nokar
serve verb	پیش کرنا	paysh karnaa
Service	خدمت	khidmat
Sesame	تل	til
Set	رکھنا	rakhnaa
Seven	سات	saat
Seventeen	سترہ	satra
Seventy	ستر	sattar
Several	بہت سے	bohot say
Severe	شدید	shadeed
Sew	سینا	sina
Sex	جنس	jins

sex verb; intercourse	مباشرت	mubasharat
sexy adjective	شہوت انگیز	shahwat angez
Shade	سایہ	saya
Shadow	سایہ	saya
shafiq noun; name	شفیق	shafiq
shahid noun; name	شاہد	shahid
Shall	کروں گا	karun gaa
Shame	شرم	sharam
shamraiz name meaning	شمریذ	shamraiz
Share	حصہ	hissa
shazeel noun; name	شاذیل	shazeel
She	وہ	wo
sheep noun; animal	بھیڑ	bherh
Shelter	پناہ	panaah
Shield	ڈھال	dhaal
Shift	بدلی	badli
Shine	چمکنا	chamakna

Ship	جہاز	jahaz
Shirt noun	کمیز	kameez
Shit noun	گندگی	gandagi
Shoe	جوتا	juta
Shoes	جوتے	jutay
Shop	دکان	dukan
Shore	ساحل	sahil
Short	چھوٹا	chota
Should	چاہئے	chahiay
Shout verb	چیخنا	cheekhna
Show	دکھانا	dikhana
Shrimp	جھینگا	jheenga
Shrub	جھاڑی	jharee
Shut	بند کرنا	band karna
Shy	شرمیلا	sharmila
Sibling	بہن بھائی	behen bhaai
Sick	مریض	mareez

Sickness	مرض	marz
side noun	کنارہ	kinara
side noun	سمت	simt
Siege	قبضہ	qabza
Sight	نظارہ	nazaara
Sign	اشارہ	ishara
Signature	دستخط	dastakhat
Significance	اہمیت	ehmiyat
Significant	نمایاں	numaya
Silence	خاموشی	khamoshi
Silent	خاموش	khamosh
Silk	ریشم	resham
Silly	بچکانا	bachkaanaa
Silver	چاندی	chandi
Similar	ملتا	milta
Simple	سادہ	sada
Simple	عام	aam

Sin	گناہ	gunaah
Since	جب سے	jab se
Sincere	مخلص	mukhlis
Sinful	گناہ گار	gunaahgar
Sing	گانا	gana
Singular	واحد	wahid
Sink	ڈوبنا	dhubna
sir noun	جناب	janaab
Sister	بہن	behn
Sit	بیٹھنا	betna
Site	جگہ	jaga
Sitting sitting	بیٹھنا	baithna
situation noun	حالت	halat
Six	چھ	chay
Sixteen	سولہ	sola
Sixty	ساٹھ	saat
Skewer noun	سیخ	seekh

Skill	ہنر	hunar
Skin noun, prevalent	جلد	jild
skinny adjective	پتلا	patla
Skirt	لہنگا	lehenga
Skull	کھوپڑی	khopri
Sky	آسمان	asmaan
Skyline	دائرہ افق	daira ufaq
slander verb; to defame	بہتان باندھنا	bohtaan bandhana
Slap	تھپڑ	thappar
Slate	سلیٹ	slate
Slave	غلام	ghulam
Sleep	سونا	sona
Sleeping verb	سونا	sona
Slight	ذرا سا	zara saa
Sloppy	بے قاعدہ	bay-qaida
Slow	آہستہ	ahista
Sly	چالاک	chalak

Small	چھوٹا	chota
Smart	چست	chust
Smell	بو	boo
Smelly	بودار	boodar
Smile noun	مسکراہٹ	muskuraahat
Smile verb	مسکرانا	muskuraana
Smoke	دھواں	dhuwan
Smooth	ہموار	hamwaar
Smooth	چکنا	chiknaa
snack noun	کھانے کی ہلکی چیز	khaanay ki halki cheez
Snake	سانپ	saanp
Snatch	چھیننا	cheenna
Sneeze verb; when a person sneezes	چھینک	cheenk
Snore	خراٹے لینا	kharaatay layna
Snores	خراٹے	kharaatay
Snow	برف	baraf
So	اس سبب	is sabab

soak verb; to make very wet in water	بگونا پانی سے	bagona
Soap noun	صابن	sabon
social adjective	ملنسار	malansar
Society	معاشره	mashara
Sock noun	جراب	jraab
Sofa	سوفا	sofa
Soft	نرم	narm
Soil	مٹی	mitti
Soldier	سپاہی	sapahi
Solid	ٹھوس	thos
Solution	حل	hal
Solve	حل کرنا	hal karna
Some	کچ	kuch
someone pronoun	کوئ ایک	koi ek
Something	کچھ	kuch
Sometimes adverb	کبھی کبھار	kabhi kabhaar
Son	بیٹا	baita

Song	گانا	gana
song noun	گانا	gana
Soon	جلد	jald
Sordid	کمینہ	kameena
Sorrow	غم	gham
Sorry	معافی مانگنا	mafi mangna
Sort noun	چھانٹنا	chhantna
Soul	روح	ruh
Sound	آواز	awaz
Soup noun	سوپ	soup
Source	منبع	mamba
South	جنوب	junoob
sovereignty noun	حکومت	hukoomat
Soybean	سویا بین	soybean
Space	خلا	khala
Spaceship	خلائی جہاز	khalai-jahaz
spam noun	فالتو	faaltu

spare noun	اکلوتا	aklota
Spark	چنگاری	chingari
Sparrow	چڑیا	chirya
Speak	کہنا	kehna
Speaker	خطیب	khateeb
Special	خاص	khaas
Specific	مخصوص	makhsoos
Speech	تقریر	taqreer
Speed	رفتار	raftaar
Spell	ہجے کرنا	hije karna
Spelling	ہجے	hijje
Spend	خرچ کرنا	kharch karna
spent verb	خرچ	kharch
Sperm noun	منی	mani
Sphere	کرہ	kurrah
Spice noun	مسالہ	masaala
Spider	مکڑی	makrhi

Spill	گرانا	girana
Spin	گھمانا	ghumana
Spinach noun	ساگ	saag
Spirit	روح	ruh
Spite	باوجود	baa-wajood
Split	شگاف	shagaaf
spoil verb; make a mess or ruin	خراب کرنا	kharab karna
Sponsor	امداد کرنے والا	imdaad karnay waalaa
Sponsor	امداد کرنا	imdaad karnaa
Spoon	چمچہ	chamcha
Spoon noun	چمچ	chamch
Sport	کھیل	khel
Sports	کھیل	khail
Spot	دھبہ	dhabba
Spouse	زوج	zoj
Spread	پھیلانا	phelana
Spring	بہار	bahaar
Spring	اچھلنا	uchalnaa

Springs	چشمہ	chashma
Sprinkle	چھڑکنا	chiranka
Spy	جاسوس	jasoos
square noun; shape	چوکور	chokor
Stability	استحکام	istehkaam
Stable	مستحکم	mustehkam
staff noun; walking aid	لاٹھی	laathi
Stairs	سیڑھی	seerhi
Stake	خطرہ	khatra
Stale	باسی	basi
Stand	کھڑے ہونا	karay hona
Standard	معیار	miyar
Star noun	تارہ	tara
Stare	گھورنا	ghoorna
Start	شروع کرنا	shuruh karna
Statement	بیان	bayaan
static adjective	ساکن	sakin

station noun	تھانہ	thana
Status	درجہ	darja
Stay	ٹھہرنا	therna
Steal	چرانا	churana
Steam	بھاپ	bhaap
Steep	ڈھلوان	dhalwaan
Step	قدم	qadam
Stick	لکڑی	lakarhi
Still adjective; unmoving	ساکت	saakit
Stimulate	ترغیب دینا	targheeb dena
stingy adjective	کنجوس	kanjoos
Stink	بدبودار	badbudar
Stipulate	مقرر کر لینا	muqarar kar lena
Stitch	ٹانکا	tanka
Stolen noun	چرا ہوا	Chura hua
Stomach	معدہ	mayda
Stone	پتھر	pathar

Stool	تپائی	tipaai
Stop	روکنا	rokna
store noun	دوکان	dukaan
Storm noun	طوفان	tufaan
Stormy	طوفانی	tofani
Story	کہانی	kahani
Stove	چولھا	chulha
Straight	سیدھا	seedha
Strange	عجیب	ajeeb
Stranger	اجنبی	ajnabee
Strawberry Noun; fruit	توت فرنگی	Tut-e-Firangi
Stream	نہر	neher
Street	سڑک	sarak
Strength	طاقت	taqat
Stress	سختی	sakhti
strict adjective	سخت	sakht
Strike noun	ہڑتال	hartaal

String	رسی	rassi
Strong	مضبوط	mazboot
Struggle	کوشش	koshish
Stubborn	ضدی	ziddi
stuck verb	پھس جانا	phas jana
Student	طالب علم	talib-e-ilm
Study	مطالعہ کرنا	mutalia karna
Stuff	اسباب	asbab
Stuffy	دم گھٹتا ہوا	dam ghuta huwa
Stun	سکتے میں لانا	sakte mein lana
Stunning	نہایت عمدہ	nihayat umda
Stupendous	عظیم الشان	azeem-us-shaan
Stupendously	حیرت انگیزی سے	hayrat-angayzi say
Stupid	بے وقوف	bay-waqoof
style noun	انداز	andaaz
Subject	مضمون	mazmoon
submit verb	بھیجنا	bhayjnaa

Subscribe	دستخط کرنا	dastakht karna
Subsequent adjective	اگلا	agla
Subtle	ہلکا	halka
Succeed	کامیاب ہونا	kamyaab hona
Success	کامیابی	kamyabi
Successful	کامیاب	kamyab
Succumb	مطیع	mutei hona
Such	جیسے	jese
Suck	چوسنا	chusna
Suckle	چسانا	chusana
Sudden	اچانک	achanak
Suffer	برداشت کرنا	bardaasht karnaa
Suffer	سہنا	sehnaa
Sufficient	کافی	kafi
Suffocate	دم گھٹنا	dam ghutna
Suffocation	گھٹن	ghutan
Sugar	شکر	shakkar
Suggest	تجویز کرنا	tajwiz karna

Suggestion	مشورہ	mashwara
Suicide	خودکشی	khud-kushi
Suitable	مناسب	munasib
Summary	خلاصہ	khulasa
Summer	موسم گرما	mosam garma
Summit	چوٹی	choti
Sun	سورج	sooraj
Sun noun	آفتاب	Aftaab
Sun noun	شمس	shams
Sunday	اتوار	itwaar
Super	بالا	bala
Superb	ذبردست	zabardast
Superficial	سطحی	sat'hi
Superintend	نگرانی کرنا	nigrani karna
Superintendent	نگران	nigran
Superior	بہتر	behter
Superiority	فضیلت	fazilat

Superlative	اعلی	aa'lah
Supersede	ہٹانا	hatana
Superstitions noun	خرافات	khoraafat
Supervise	دیکھ بال کرنا	dekh-baal karna
Supervision	نگرانی	nigrani
supper noun	رات کا کھانا	raat ka kahna
Supple	ملائم	mulaim
Support	سہارا دینا	sahara dena
Suppose	فرض کرنا	farz karna
Sure	یقین ہونا	yaqeen hona
Surf	پھین	pheen
Surface	سطح	sataah
Surprise	حیران کرنا	heraan karna
Surrender	مغلوب ہو جانا	maghloob ho jana
Surround	گھیرنا	gherna
Survive	قائم رہنا	qaim rehna
Survivor	بچا ہوا	bacha huwa
Suspect	شبہ کرنا	shuba karna

Suspicion	شک و شبہ	shak-o-shuba
Suspicious	مشکوک	mashkook
Swallow	نگلنا	nigalna
Swallow	ابابیل	abaabeel
swat noun; place	سوات	swat
Swear	قسم اٹھانا	qasam uthana
Sweat	پسینہ	paseena
Sweet	میٹھا	meetha
Sweetheart	معشوقہ	ma'shuqa
Sweetness noun	چاشنی	chaashni
Swim	تیرنا	terna
swimming verb	تیرنا	tairna
Swing verb	جھولا جھولنا	Jhola Jholna
Sword noun	تلوار	talvaar
Symbol	علامت	ilamat
Sympathetic	ہمدرد	hamdard
Sympathy	ہمدردی	hamdardi

System	نظام	nizam
Systematic	بانظام	ba-nizam

T-U-V-W

Tab	ٹکڑا	tukra
Table noun	میز	mayz
Tail	دم	dum
Tailor	درزی	darzi
Take	لینا	layna
Taking verb	لے رہا	lay reha
Tale	کہانی	kahani
Talent	ذہانت	zahanat
Talk	بات کرنا	baat karna
Tall	اونچا	ooncha
Tall adjective	بلند	buland
Tame	پالتو	paltu
Tangle	الجھنا	ulajhna
Task	کام	kaam
Taste	چکھنا	chakhna

Taste noun	ذوق	zouq
tasty adjective	لذیذ	laziz
Tea	چائے	chai
Teach	سکھانا	sikhana
Teacher	استاد	ustaad
Teaching	تربیت	tarbiyat
Tear	آنسو	ansoo
Tease	ستانا	satana
Technology	ٹیکنالجی	technology
Teeth	دانت	daant
Telephone	ٹیلی فون	telephone
Telescope	دوربین	durbeen
Tell	بتانا	batana
Temper	غضب	ghazab
Temperature	درجہ حرارت	darja hararat
Temple	مندر	mandir
temporary adjective; any temporary thing	عارضی	aarzi

Tempt	اکسانا	uksana
Temptation adjective	لالچ	Lalach
Ten	دس	das
Tend	رجحان	rujhan
Tent	شامیانہ	shamyana
Tentative	امتحانا	imtehanan
Term	مدت	muddat
Terrible	بہت برا	bohot bura
Terrific	زبردست	zabardast
Terrify	ڈرانا	darana
Territory	سلطنت	saltanat
Terror	خوف	khof
terrorism noun	دہشت گردی	dehshat gardi
Test	امتحان	imtehan
Testament	انجیل	injeel
Testament	تورات	toraah
Testimonial	تعریف	tareef

testimony noun	گواہی	gavaahi
Thank	شکریہ ادا کرنا	shukria ada karna
Thankful	شکرگزار	shukar guzar
Thanks	شکریہ	shukria
Thankyou	شکریہ	shukria
That	وہ	woh
thee pronoun; for you	تمہارے لیے	tumhaaray liye
Theft	چوری	chori
Their	ان کا	un ka
Them	ان کو	un ko
Themself	خود	khud
Then	پھر	phir
There	وہاں	wahan
Thereby adverb	اس کے سبب	is kay sabab
Therefore	پس	pas
These	یہ	ye
They	وہ	woh

Thick thick liquid	گاڑھا	Gaarha
Thief	چور	choer
Thin	پتلا	patlaa
Thing noun	چیز	cheez
Think	سوچنا	soch naa
Thinking verb	سوچنا	sochna
Third adjective	تیسری	theesri
Thirst	پیاس	piyas
Thirsty	پیاسا	piyasa
Thirteen	تیرہ	tayra
Thirty	تیس	tees
This	یہ	yeh
Thorn	کانٹا	kaantaa
Those	ان	un
Thought	خیال	khiyal
Thoughtful	پرفکر	pur-fikar

Thousand noun	ہزار	hazaar
Thread	دھاگہ	dhaga
Threat	دھمکی	dhumki
Three	تین	teen
Thrill	جوش	josh
Throat noun	گلہ	galla
throne noun	حکومت	hukoomat
Through	بدولت	badolat
Throw	پھینکنا	phenkna
Thrust	دھکہ	dhakka
Thunder	گرج	garj
Thursday	جمعرات	jume-raat
Thus	اسسبب	is-sabab
Tickle noun	گدگدی	gudgudee
tidy clean	ستھرا	sutra
Tie	باندھنا	baandhna
Tiger	شیر	sher

Till	تک	tak
Time	وقت	waqt
Timetable	ٹایم ٹیبل	timetable
Tiny	بہت چھوٹا	bohot chota
Tired	تھکا ہوا	thaka huwa
Tits noun; vulgar	چھاتیاں	chaatian
To	طرف	taraf
Tobacco	تمباکو	tambaku
Today	آج	aaj
Toe	انگھوٹا	anghuta
Together	سات	saath
Toilet	بیت الخلا	bayt-ul-khala
Told verb	بتایا	bataayaa
Tolerate	برداشت کرنا	bardaasht karnaa
Tomorrow	کل	kal
Tongue	زبان	zabaan
Tonight today night	آج رات	Aaj Raat

Too	بھی	bhi
Took verb; past tense	لے لیا	lay lia
Tool	اوزار	auzaar
Tools	آلات	aalaat
Tooth	دانت	daanth
Top	اوپر	oopar
Tornado	طوفان	tufaan
Torture	اذیت	aziyat
Toss	پھینکنا	phenkna
Total	مکمل	mukammal
Totally	مکمل طور پر	mukamal-tor-par
Touch	چھونا	chuna
Tough	سخت	sakht
tourism noun	سیر و سیاحت	sayr-o-siyaahat
Tow	کھینچنا	khenchna
Town	قصبہ	qasba
Toy	کھلونا	khilona

Trade noun	تجارت	tijarat
Tradition noun	روایت	rivaayat
Traditional adjective	راویتی	rawaiti
Train	تربیت دینا	tarbiyat dena
traitor traitor	غدار	ghaddar
Transaction	معملہ	ma'mla
Transfer	منتقل کرنا	muntaqil karna
Translate	ترجمہ کرنا	tarjuma karna
Translation	ترجمہ	tarjuma
Transport	ذریعہ سفر	zarya-e-safr
Transportation	مواصلات	muwasilat
Trap	جال	jaal
Trash	ردی چیز	radi cheez
Trash	بے کار	baykaar
Travel	سفر کرنا	safar karna
traveler noun	مسافر	musaafir
Traveller noun	مسافر	musaafir

Treason	غداری	gaddari
Treasure	خزانہ	khazana
Treatment	علاج	ilaaj
Tree	درخت	darakht
tremble verb	لرز جانا	laraz jaanaa
Tremendous	بہت زیادہ	bohot ziyada
Tress	زلف	zulf
Trial	آزمائیش	azmaish
Tribute	خراج	khiraj
Trifle	تھوڑا سا	thora sa
Trip	سفر	safar
Trouble	مصیبت	museebat
True	سچا	sachcha
trunk noun; elephant trunk	سونڈ	soond
Trust	اعتماد	itemaad
Truth	سچ	sach
Try	کوشش کرنا	koshish karna

Tuesday	منگل	mangal
Turkey noun; animal	فیل مرغ	feel-murgh
turmeric noun; south asian spice	ہلدی	haldi
Turn	مڑنا	murna
Turnip noun; vegetable	شلجم	shaljum
Tutor	اتالیق	ataleeq
Tutor	ٹیوٹر	tutor
Tutorial	سبق	sabaq
Twelve	بارہ	bara
Twenty	بیس	bees
twice noun	دو مرتبہ	do mertaba
Two	دو	do
type noun	طرح	tarah
Ugly	بدصورت	badsoorat
Ultimate	آخری	akhri
Ultimately	آخرکار	akhirkaar
Umbrella	چھتری	chhatri

Unable	ناقابل	na-qabil
Uncle	انکل	uncle
Uncle noun; paternal uncle	چچا	chacha
Uncle noun; maternal uncle	ماموں	mamoon
Uncle noun; paternal aunts husband	پھوپا	phuppa
Uncle noun; maternal aunts husband	خالو	khalu
Uncle noun; elder paternal uncle	تایا	taya
Uncomfortable	بےآرام	bay aaraam
unconditional adjective	غیر مشروط	ghair mashroot
Unconscious	بےہوش	bay hosh
Under	نیچے	neechay
Underground	زیر زمین	zayray zameen
Understand	سمجھنا	samajna
Understanding	سمجھ	samajh
Undo	کھولنا	kholna
unemployed verb	بے روزگار	berozgaar
Ungrateful	ناشکرگزار	naa shukarguzaar

Unhappy	ناخوش	naa khush
Union	انجمن	anjuman
Unique	منفرد	munfarid
Unit	اکائی	ikaai
Unite	اکٹھا کرنا	ikhatta karna
Unity	اتحاد	itehad
Universe	کائنات	kaainaat
University	جامعہ	jamia
Unknown	نامعلوم	na-ma'loom
Unknown adjective	انجانی	anjaani
unless conjunction	سیوا	sivaa
Unload	اتارنا	utarna
Until	جب تک	jab tak
Up	اوپر	upar
Update	جدید بنانا	jadeed banana
Upload	چڑھانا	charhana
Upper	اوپرکا	upar-ka

Upset	پریشان کرنا	parayshan karna
Uranus	یورینس	uranus
Urdu	اردو	urdu
Urduword	اردو لفظ	urdu lafz
Urduword	اردوورڈکام	urduword
Urgent	ضروری	zaruri
Urine	پیشاب	pishab
Us	ہمیں	hamein
Use	استعمال کرنا	istemaal karna
useful adjective	کارآمد	karaamad
Useless	غیرضروری	ghair zaruri
Usman name	عثمان	usman
Usually	اکثر	aksar
Usurp verb	غصب کر نا	gasb karna
Utensil	برتن	bartan
Utmost	بےحد	bay-had
Utopia	یوٹوپیا	utopia

Utter verb	الفاظ اگلنا	alfaaz ugalnaa
Vacant	خالی	khali
Vacate	خالی کرنا	khali karna
Vagina noun; a female organ	فرج	furj
Vaginal adjective	فرج کا	furj kaa
Vague adjective	غیرواضع	ghair waaze
Vain	لاحاصل	la-hasil
Valley	وادی	waadi
Value	قیمت	qeemat
Vanish	غائب ہونا	ghaib hona
Vanity noun	غرور	ghuroor
Vanquish verb	مکمل شکست دینا	mukammal shikasht dena
Vapour	بخارات	bukharat
Variable	بدلنے والا	badalnay-wala
Variance	تبدیلی	tabdeeli
Variant	مختلف	mukhtalif
Various	مختلف	mukhtalif

Vary	مختلف	mukhtalif
Vase	دان	guldaan
Vast	وسیع	wasee
Vegetable	سبزی	sabzee
Vehicle	سواری	sawaari
Veil	نقاب	niqaab
Vein	ورید	vareed
Vendor	بیچنے والا	bechnay-wala
Vendor	دکان دار	dukaan daar
Venerable	معزز	mo'azzaz
Venerate	عزت کرنا	izzat karna
Veneration	عزت	izzat
Venom	زہر	zeher
Ventilator	روشندان	roshandan
Venus	زہرہ	zuhra
Veranda	برآمدہ	baramada
Verb part of speech	فعل	fayl

Verbal	زبانی	zabani
Version	تبدیل صورت	tabdeel-e-soorat
Vertical	عمودی	amudi
Very	بہت	bohot
Vice	نائب	naib
Vicious	ظالم	zaalim
Victim	مظلوم	mazloom
Victory	فتح	fatah
Video	وڈیو	video
View	منظر	manzar
Village	گاؤں	gaaon
Violation	خلاف ورزی	khilaf-warzi
Violence	تشدد	tashdud
Violent	شدید	shadeed
Virgin	کنواری	kunwari
Virtual	خیالی	khiyali
Visible	دکھائی دیتا	dikhaai dayta
Vision	نظر	nazar

visit verb	دورہ	daurah
Visitor	ملاقاتی	mulaqati
Vista noun	منظر	manzar
Vivid	واضح	wazeh
Vocabulary	ذخیرہ الفاظ	zakheera e alfaaz
Voice	آواز	aawaz
Void	خالی	khali
Volcano	آتشفشاں	aatish-fishaan
Volume	حجم	hujam
volunteer noun	رضاکار	razakaar
vomit noun	الٹی	ulti
Vow	عہد کرنا	ehed karna
Voyage	سفر	safar
vulgar adjective	گنوار	ghanwar
Vulnerable	غیر محفوظ	gher mahfooz
waist noun	کمر	kamar
Wait	انتظار کرنا	intezar karna

Wake	جاگنا	jagna
wakeup verb	اٹھنا	uthnaa
Walk	چلنا	chalna
Wall	دیوار	diwaar
walnut noun; dry fruit	اخروٹ	akhrot
walter noun; name	والٹر	walter
wander verb	پھرنا	phirna
Wanna	چاہتا	chaahtaa
Want	چاہنا	chaahna
wanted verb	مطلوب	matloob
waqar noun; guy name	وقار	waqar
waqas noun; name	وقاص	waqas
War	جنگ	jang
Warehouse	گودام	godaam
Warm	گرم	garm
Warn	آگاہ	aagah
Was verb; male	تھا	thaa

Was verb; female	تھی	thee
waseem noun; name	وسیم	waseem
Wash	دھونا	dhona
wasif noun; guy name	واصف	wasif
Wasp	بھڑ	bhir
Waste	ضایع کرنا	zaya karna
Watch	گھڑی	gharhi
Watch	دیکھنا	daykhna
Water	پانی	pani
watermelon noun; fruit	تربوز	tarbooz
Wave	لہر	leher
Way	راستہ	raasta
We	ہم	hum
Weak	کمزور	kamzor
wealth noun	دولت	daulat
Wear	پہننا	pehenna
Weather	موسم	mosam

Web	جالا	jala
Website	ویب سائٹ	website
Wed	شادی کرنا	shadi karna
Wedding	شادی	shadi
Wedlock	نکاح	nikah
Wednesday	بدھ	budh
Weed	گھاس	ghaas
Week	ہفتہ	hafta
weep verb	رونا	ronaa
Weigh	وزن کرنا	wazan karna
Weight	وزن	wazan
Weird	عجیب	ajeeb
Welcome	خوش امدید	khush amdeed
Well	کنواں	kunwan
Went	گیا	giaa
Were	تھے	thay
West	مغرب	maghrib

Wet	بھیگا ہوا	bhiga huwa
What	کیا	kia
Whatever	جو بھی	jo bhi
Wheat noun	گندم	gandum
Wheel	پہیہ	payya
When	کب	kab
whenever conjunction; whenever there is a problem	جب بھی	jab bhi
Where	کہاں	kahan
Whether	چاہے	chaahay
Which	کونسا	konsa
While	جب	jab
Whimsical adjective	من موجی	man moji
Whisper	سرگوشی کرنا	sargooshi karna
White	سفید	safed
Who	کون	kon
whole adjective; feminine	پوری	puri

whole adjective; feminine	پورا	poora
Whom	جس کو	jis ko
Whomever	جو بھی	jo bhi
whore noun	رنڈی	randi
Whose	کس کا	kiska
Why	کیوں	kiyoon
Wide	چوڑا	chorha
widow noun	بیوہ	baiwah
Wield	انتظام	intezam
Wife	بیوی	beewee
Wild	جنگلی	jangli
Will	کرے گا	kare ga
Will verb; female first person	کروں گی	karoon gi
will verb; male first person	کروں گا	karoon ga
Willing	رضامند	razamand
Willingness	رضامندی	razamandi
Wimple	نقاب	niqaab

Win	جیتنا	jeetna
Wind	چلتی ہوا	chalti hawa
Window	کھڑکی	khirki
Wine	شراب	sharab
Wing	پر	par
wink verb	آنکھ جھپکنا	ankh jhapakna
Winning	کامیاب	kamyab
Winter	موسم سرما	mosam sarma
Wire	تار	taar
Wisdom	عقل	aqal
Wise	عقلمند	aqalmand
Wish	خواہش	khuwaahish
Wishes	خواہشات	khuwahishat
Wishful	خواہش مند	khuwaahish- mand
Witch	چڑیل	churail
With	ساتھ	saath
Withdraw	ہٹا لینا	hata lena

Without	بغیر	baghayr
witness verb	شہادت	shahaadat
Wolf prevalent	بھیڑیا	bheyrya
Woman	عورت	oarat
Women noun	عورتیں	aurtain
Wonder	حیران ہونا	heran hona
Wonderful	حیران کن	hairan kun
Wonderful adjective	قابل تعریف	qaabil-e-taarif
Wont verb	نہیں کرے گا	nahee karay ga
Wood	لکڑی	lakarhi
Wool	اون	oon
Word	لفظ	lafz
Work	کام	kaam
Worker	مزدور	mazdoor
working adjective	کام	kaam
Workshop	کارخانہ	karkhana
World	دنیا	duniya

world noun	جہاں	jahan
Worried adjective	پریشان	parayshaan
Worry	فکر	fikar
worse adjective	برا	bura
Worship verb	عبادت	ibaadat
Worst	بدترین	bad-tareen
Worth	قابل	qabil
Would as in phrase "she/they/you would"	کریں گی	karayn gee
Would as in phrase "would be"	ہو گا	ho ga
Would as in phrase "he/they/you would"	کریں گے	karayn gay
Would as in question "would you (female)..."	کیا آپ کریں گی	kiyaa aap karayn gee
Would as in question "would you (male)..."	کیا آپ کریں گے	kiyaa aap karayn gay
Wound	زخم	zakham
Wow	واہ	wah
Wrap	لپٹنا	lipatna
Wreck	ٹوٹنا پھوٹنا	tootna phutna

Wreckage	ٹوٹی پھوٹی حالت	tooti phuti halat
Wrench	اچانک کھینچ لینا	achanak kench lena
Wrench	رینچ	wrench
Wring	نچوڑنا	nichorna
Wrinkle	شکن	shikan
Wrist	کلائی	kalai
Write	لکھنا	likhna
Writing noun	لکھائی	likhai
Written	لکھاہوا	likha hua
Wrong	غلط	galat
Wrote	لکھا	likha
Wrung	نچوڑنا	nichorna
Wry	منہ لٹکانا	moon latkana

X – Y – Z

xerox verb	کاپی کرنا	copy karnaa
Yacht	چھوٹی کشتی	choti kishti
yaman noun; country	یمان	yaman
Yank	کھینچنا	khenchna
Yard	گز	gaz
Yard	صحن	sehen
Yarn	سوت	soot
Yawl	چھوٹی کشتی	choti kishti
yawn noun	جماھی	jamaahi
Yea	ہاں	haan
Yeah	ہاں	haan
Year	سال	saal
Year noun	سن	san
Yeast	خمیر	khameer
Yell	چیخنا	cheekhna
Yellow	پیلا	peela

Yellow adjective	زرد	zard
Yellow noun	زرد	zard
Yelp verb	اچانک چیخ مارنا	achanak cheekh maarna
Yen	جاپانی کرنسی	yen
Yes	جی ہاں	jee haan
yes noun	ہاں	haan
Yesterday	کل	kal
Yet	اس کے باوجود	is ke bawajood
Yet	ابھی تک	abhi tak
Yield	حاصل کردا	hasil karda
Yoghurt	دہی	dahi
yogurt noun	دہی	dahi
Yolk	زردی	zardi
You	آپ	aap
You noun; informal	تم	tum
younas noun; name	یونس	younas
Young	جوان	jawaan

Youngster	بچہ	bacha
Your pronoun; male object	آپ کا	aap ka
Your pronoun; female	آپ کی	aap ki
Yourself	آپ خود	aap khud
yousaf noun; name	یوسف	yousaf
Youth	جوانی	jawani
Yowl	چیخنا	cheekhna
Yule	کرسمس	christmas
zafar noun; name	ظفر	zafar
Zara name	زارا	zara
zardari noun; name	زرداری	zardari
Zeal	اشتیاق	ishteyak
Zealous	شوقین	shokeen
Zebra	زیبرا	zebra
Zenith	سمت الراس	simturraas
Zero	صفر	sifar
Zest	مزا	maza

Zigzag	پیچ دار	paych daar
Zip	ذپ	zip
Zone	علاقہ	ilaqa
Zoo	چڑیاگھر	chirya ghar
Zoology	علم الحیوانات	ilm-ul-hewanat
Zoom	تیزی سے آنا	taizi se ana
Zoroastrian	آتش پرست	aatish parast
Zoroastrianism	مزہب زرتشت	mazhab-e-zartusht
zubair noun; name	زبیر	zubair